HIGH ROAD RIDER

HIGH ROAD RIDER

By Mike Hannan

CONTENTS

The Alps and the Detour

France

Switzerland

Altdorf

Geneva

Grenoble

Milan

Carpentras

Nice

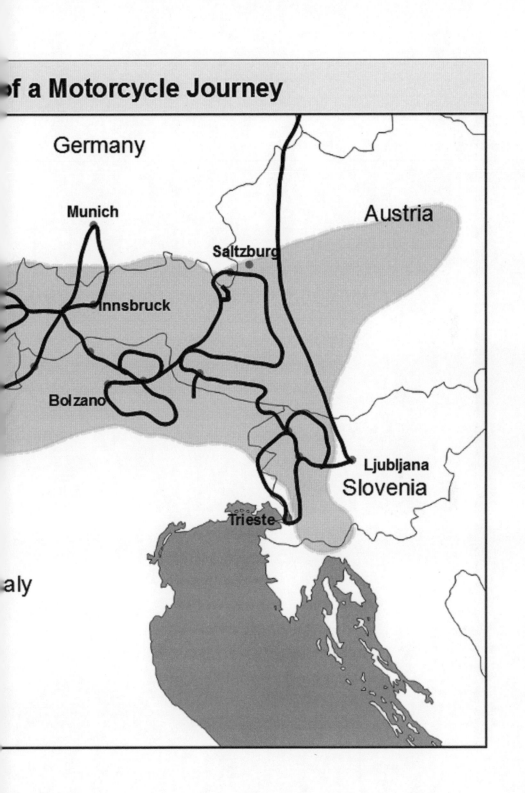

1

THE LURE OF THE MOUNTAINS

On a cold day in late September, in a pass high in the Swiss Alps, I pulled my motorcycle into a siding. As I waited for my wife, Jo, to climb down from the back seat, I looked around the bleak and forlorn landscape. The Furkapass, 2429m, was certainly nothing much to look at. It lacked the rugged beauty of many alpine passes, and although it was one of the higher passes in Switzerland, the road up had been undemanding. The brooding black clouds rolling in from the west gave it the sort of sinister feel we like to avoid, and we still had long way to go in the fading light of the afternoon.

Despite this inauspicious first impression, we took our time to look around. I climbed the hill behind the park to look for somewhere to take a photograph. We walked down the road in both directions, searching for a view beyond the mountains, then sat on a fence to watch a few motorcycles glide past. Later, when we looked back, it seemed a strange place to start our exploration of the Alps.

Jo and I are experienced motorcycle travellers. In the past, we have ridden across North Africa, Russia and Mongolia and spent a year living off the back of our bike. In recent years, drawn back to London by our first granddaughter, we have continued to ride, criss-crossing Europe so many times that our maps look as though they've been hashed with highlighter pen.

It is, in many ways, a demanding way to travel. On a bike, you are exposed to the elements, the vagaries of the roads and the folly of fellow road users. On a bike, there is nowhere to hide. If it is hot, you swelter; if it rains, you get 'wet; and the biting cold of winter can leave your fingers aching in minutes. On the worst days, rain, cold, cross winds, ice, hail and fog take their turns to make each hour in the saddle a trial of perseverance.

It also has its own delights and joys. On a motorcycle, our lives are disentangled from our usual world, to the extent that everything that matters to us can be packed into a couple of small bags. Everything we need to survive is within arm's reach. The average backpacker carries twice as much, but on a bike there is nowhere to pack anything more and, since we have no space, no need to purchase anything new. Our motto—if you buy a tissue, throw out a tissue—is more than a cute adage. On the road, it is the simple rule we live by, and gives the journey an elegant, joyful logic. You don't need stuff to be happy.

Then there is the motorcycle itself. Each bike we have owned has had a personality as distinctive as any living creature, and our relationship with each one has been a familiar mix of pleasure and forbearance. We remember a Ducati that just stopped (possibly for a cappuccino), an AJS that thumped its way to and from work with grim determination, an Indian Chief as tough and reliable as when it was built in 1944, and our BMW R1150GS Adventure, known as Elephant. Even the bike we used on this journey, a Suzuki DL 1000, purchased second-hand in London, had a special character all its own: she is plain, reliable and sure-footed. For us, every motorcycle journey involves three parties, all of whom need to work together. Each has distinct but overlapping responsibilities, vital to the survival of the whole, and in the end our rolling mass is almost a single entity: 450kg of aluminium, flesh, steel and Cordura. It is an ungainly mix of human and machine. In part, it is this synergy that structures our lives and makes our journey special.

Whatever our feelings towards our machines, it is the way motorcycles work on the road that keeps us riding, and is often such a mystery to non-riders. At the heart of a motorcycle in motion is an impossible balance of forces that keep it from falling to the ground, no matter how far it leans into a corner, and hurl it along at breathtaking speed. When it all works, when the weather is right, when the road is an endless series of sweeping corners, when the great god of horsepower smiles, the riding transcends mere travel and becomes a joy in itself. These are the diamond days, and whether they happen in the Atlas mountains of Morocco or on the Great Ocean Road in Australia, they are compensation, a thousand times over, for the misery of traffic and rain.

It was the search for perfect motorcycle roads that took us around the world and eventually brought us to that barren pass in the mountains. With our offspring grown, Jo and I had moved interstate to a warmer climate and started to behave like the 'empty nesters' we were. The changes didn't go unnoticed to our children, and as is usually the case, they were one step in front of us. One Christmas, they gave us a copy of John Hermann's *Motorcycle Journeys through the Alps and Corsica* and Chris Scot's *Adventure Motorcycling Handbook*. From there, our life spiralled out of control. A year later we found ourselves in a transport depot in Wembley, outside London, unpacking the bike we would call Elephant from a crate.

That was September 2007. A year later, we packed Elephant into another crate, in another depot, this time in Gimpo, South Korea. The story of how we got there became my first book, *The Elephant's Tale*. That year on the road was supposed to be the catharsis that cleared away the cobwebs of working life, and gave us a renewed zest for our careers, but it didn't work quite like that. We didn't feel refreshed—we just felt changed. There was no going back to our old lives and we immediately started planning our next adventure.

In the end, all of this was titillation ahead of our eventual seduction by the Alps. We had, of course, always known about the Alps, in that imprecise way that people know about famous stuff on the other side of the world. It was the sort of abstract understanding that framed places like the Great Wall of China or the Russian Steppes for a boy growing up in an impoverished suburb of post-war Sydney. In my case, an appreciation of the Alps probably didn't amount to much more than the knowledge that they were high mountains in Switzerland where rich people liked to ski and climb and wear funny hats. But then, people wear funny hats in lots of places. I had also studied Latin at school, a highly structured waste of time for a working class lad, and I knew that Hannibal had crossed the Alps with elephants.

This didn't add much to my understanding, as the Alps were north of Rome and modern-day Italy, while Carthage was on the other side of the Mediterranean to the south. It was another of those mysteries to make the young shrug their shoulders, turning away to the window and more interesting daydreams.

Over the years, constant travel had rolled back the mystery of many remote places, but it was only our immersion in the world of adventure motorcycling that finally set our course for the mountains. As we started to meet other long distance riders and read their travel stories, the Alps appeared again and again, and we started to understand that this was a place where nature and man had conspired to make a paradise for motorcyclists. All the while, John Hermann's book sat undisturbed on our bookshelf until one day, after a conversation over coffee about where we might go next, Jo took it down and started to read. Bookmarks and margin notes appeared, maps were laid out on the dining room table, and other references joined the pile. Travel guides, more maps, political and cultural histories, some dating back 150 years, magazine articles and a seemingly endless list of websites produced a flow of new information and set off that familiar yearning to get back on the road.

The first problem, however, was an unexpectedly simple one. Where exactly were 'the Alps'? Everyone talked about them as though they were just there and you couldn't miss them. You know, go to southern France and head east. Our large-scale map of Europe had the word 'ALPEN' stamped across the bottom of Austria, in such bold print that it was obviously intended to indicate that THIS was the place. But there were mountains everywhere. Which ones were 'the Alps', and which were just incidental alps? Like a lot of simple questions, this one hid a wider truth. The Alps have always been more than a long range of mountains, regardless of which mountains were considered to comprise them, and they have a deeper significance that is central to the nature of modern Europe and its tumultuous history. Intertwined with the mountains are core beliefs about identity, nation and culture, as relevant today as they were 2,000 years ago when a stabilising Roman republic sheltered behind the mountains from the tribes of the dark forested plains to the north.

The nature of these mountains, however, goes back 250 million years, to when the area we now call the Alps was a vast shallow sea. Layers of sand and clay laid the foundation of sandstone, shale and limestone that is the basis of much of today's range. At this time, magnesium-rich dolomite was formed, which later defined the mountains of the same name, and the limestone plateaus of the French Alps were consolidated. The area remained buried until about 65 million years ago, when the movement of the great plates of disintegrating supercontinents came together. The African plate collided with the Eurasian plate in one of those cataclysmic, slow motion dramas that formed our world, and started the process of creating modern Europe. The collision thrust up the land along the join, pushing up the mineral-rich strata from deep below the sea. Outcrops of gneiss found on San Bernardino Pass in Switzerland were once buried 100km below the surface.

Many geologists have spent their lives trying to unravel the mysteries of alpine structure and a good part of the 19th century was taken up with the task of 'rock mapping'. Understanding and explaining what happened to create these mountains has been a still longer and more complex task. As the great geologist

Richard Fortey explains it, 'this region of the earth's crust is where everything is topsy-turvy, where great slabs of rock may be flipped over like badly-tossed pancakes, and where a mountain of a height to challenge the most experienced alpinist may be no more than the tip of a vast geological fold.'[1] Like so much else about the Alps, its geology is so complex, it defies simple explanation.

The African plate still pushes north a few millimetres each year. In a high valley above Bellinzona, in the Swiss canton of Ticino, the knowledgeable traveller can stand on a bridge over the Mobbio River and straddle the fault line where the two plates meet. The mountains we call the Alps form a 1000km arc along that European–African divide. They run from the French Mediterranean coast across Switzerland, through the bottom of Austria and Germany and the north of Italy, finally tapering out in the plains of northern Slovenia. The Alps are part of a wider group of mountains, known as the Alptide Belt, which spans the fault where the Eurasian plate meets not only the African plate but also the Arabian and Indian plates. The Alptide Belt runs all the way from Indonesia through Central Asia and Southern Europe and out into the Atlantic Ocean. As well as the Alps, it includes the Carpathians, the mountains of Anatolia and Iran, the Hindu Kush and the mountains of South-East Asia.

The geology of the Alps has also been central to the lives of its people, this human history being as fragmented as the geology. For most of history, life in the Alps was relentlessly hard and governed by the complex nature of the mountains. High, rocky valleys, poor soils leached of nutrient, the endless cycle of following livestock up and down the mountains with the seasons, known as transhumance, and the brutal climate all made life here a struggle. That the mountains are now made prosperous by 200 years of tourism doesn't change the simple truth that they have always been a hard place to scratch out a living.

As the wave of humanity swept out of Africa, the Alps were among the last places to be settled. New technology was needed to survive in the mountains. At the least, our ancestors needed warm clothing, and the ability to control fire and build effective shelters. There is evidence that our Neanderthal cousins occupied alpine caves 50,000 years ago, but the oldest Neanderthal sites in Europe are 300,000 years old. For a predator like the Neanderthal, life in the Alps would have been linked to the migration of grazing herds, the same cycle of transhumance that has always governed life in the mountains.

The oldest rock art to be discovered in the Alps so far and attributed to modern man dates back about 8,000 years. The anthropologists are still undecided about how our ancestors coexisted with the Neanderthals for thousands of years, and the extent to which the two species competed, cooperated and interbred. What is clear, however, is that modern man has been adapting to the Alps for at least 10,000 years. The discovery in 1991 of a Neolithic man preserved in ice on the Similaun Glacier was a dramatic indication of how well our own ancestors had met the challenge of the mountains. Ötzi, as he came to be called, had well-made shoes and goat-skin clothing, a warm hat made of bear skin, and a backpack with food and the means to make fire. His reason for being in the mountains remains uncertain, but his level of preparedness is clear.

Eventually, people left a more lasting record. The Iron Age Celts, my own ancestral link to the Alps, swept in from central Europe and spread over much of western continental

Europe, the Iberian Peninsula, Ireland and Britain. The Celts' occupation was displaced by the Romans and later by the waves of Germanic tribes. Some small pockets of Celtic descendants remain in the Alps. Throughout the Dark Ages and Middle Ages (from 1066 CE), the populations of the Alps were constantly displaced and replaced, as the fractured nature of the land restricted communications and resulted in confusing power struggles and shifting allegiances.

Despite this long human history, the Alps have also been seen as a place of fear and mystery, home to isolated, fearsome and independent peoples, mythical monsters and legendary heroes— not a place for civilised folk. During the 17th and 18th centuries, as nation states slowly coalesced out of the feudal Dark Ages, the Alps were among the last places to be subsumed into expanding empires and have remained a stronghold of regional identity, even as borders have shifted and nations emerged. Today, the place is an intoxicating mix of cultures and languages, and uncertain and regional allegiances. It is a place where a veneer of modern national identity often hides differences that go back to an ancient past.

The Alps create a divide between the distinctive cultures of the north and south of Europe—to the north, Germany, economic success and industrial efficiency; to the south, Italy, with a different culture, different economy and different prospects for the future. The people of the Alps are a bridge between these two faces of Europe, often possessing a stake in each culture, with loyalty divided between nation and family. For a traveller with an eye to these detail, it is a fascinating mix.

It was this history that eventually brought us to desolate Furkapass, on a bleak day, with our now dog-eared and annotated copy of John Hermann's book in our saddlebag. A few kilometres further west through the pass, the waters of the Rhône Glacier were melting and running into streams, which tumbled out of the mountains to the south and cascaded down into the mighty Rhône. The waters of the Rhône flowed strong with the summer melt, rolling brown and wide through a land of wine and sunshine and olives, south to the Mediterranean. A few kilometres behind us, water also raced down through the mountain tributaries and on to the Rhine, then north through the endless plains of central Europe, through lands of beer and root vegetables and bitter winters, all the way to the icy waters of the Baltic.

This unprepossessing pass was a watershed, a place where water flowed into different systems, through different lands, different climates and different cultures. It was a place where worlds separated. This seemed worth a few minutes of contemplation. Though strange and bleak, it was a fitting place to start our story.

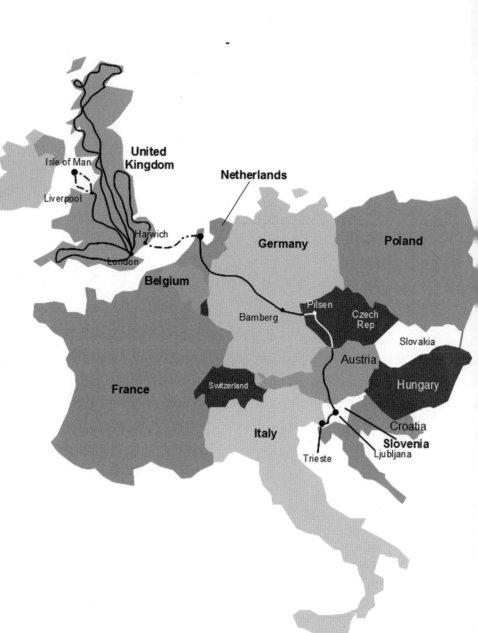

2

A SLOW START TO A LONG SUMMER

ike all good plans, our approach to the Alps was simple, or at least started out that way. Rather than ship Elephant to Europe, we decided to buy a second-hand bike in the UK, using our daughter's London residence as a registration address. We would then ride it around the Alps for a few years before we sold it and moved on to other adventures. Finding a bike online was easy. It was just as easy to buy and take possession of a 2003 Suzuki DL 1000. Getting a company to insure it to be ridden on a foreign licence was, however, an expensive nightmare, more difficult and expensive than getting insurance for our foreign registered bike, Elephant, two years previously.

We approached this problem the way we had learned to deal with all our problems on the road, persevering with bloody-minded determination until we found a way through. Many would think the insurance hurdle should have been foreseen, and a different approach taken in the first place, but from our experience over-planning causes more problems that it solves for adventure travel. You need to know that your plan is workable but you can't solve every problem before you start. If you get lost in the maze of detail, you will become overwhelmed and give up. It is likely that more adventures are stillborn because of this than fail once underway due to a lack of planning.

The bike had attractive blue paint and was in a generally good condition, with low mileage for its age. It lacked a few necessary features for its role with us, but after a week of toiling in the front yard of a tiny London terrace, it started to look the part. Large side panniers and a back-box came with the bike and provided most of the carrying capacity. We added a very large tank bag which was mounted with some special, home made, fixing points. We needed heated handgrips to help keep the cold at bay, and purchased and fitted a taller windscreen and centre stand. It took a day of cursing (providing much amusement for the neighbours) to wire in our Garmin GPS and intercom system, both of which had been transferred from Elephant. I also found two excellent small packs, the type used on bicycles, which I modified to fit onto the front crash bars of the bike. These and the tank bag allowed some of the weight of the load to be shifted forward to improve the balance and handling of the bike.

There were a few other little fixtures and fittings needed, but by the time we rolled out of London on our way to Scotland for a shakedown run, we were very happy with how the new bike had come together. Everything was neatly stowed and the weight distribution was excellent. Once we were in wilds of the West

Highlands, she was flying, and we had a great time exploring back roads and eating wild salmon.

Back in London, we fitted new tyres, a chain and sprocket set, and an automatic chain oiler. We were ready to roll. Well ... not quite. The bike had a shudder in the clutch that was becoming very annoying. It was, I discovered, a common problem with that year model and had been solved in later years by a modified design of the clutch basket. It wouldn't affect the bike's reliability, but it took some of the fun out of riding. I priced a clutch basket and the necessary bits and pieces locally, but they were too expensive to make the job worthwhile, and with a little more work I discovered I could get the parts out of the US or Australia at less than half the UK price. I decided that I would bring the parts with me on the next trip, and this, in retrospect, is where the wheels (almost literally) fell off.

We found our way out of London again, this time headed for 10 days on the Isle of Man for the TT Racing. The annual motorcycle races on the Isle of Man, known as the Tourist Trophy or TT, are legendary. First run in 1907 and won that year by Charlie Collier on a Matchless, it was the most prestigious motorcycle race in the world championship for many years, and remains extraordinarily challenging and dangerous. The difficult 54km course takes years to learn, running on public roads along country lanes and through towns and villages, with no safety run-offs and no room for error. More than 260 racers have died in the TT and many hundreds of others have been seriously injured. Only the very brave are willing to race at the Isle of Man.

I had grown up on stories of the TT. The great racing heroes of my boyhood, Giacomo Agostini and Mike Hailwood, were both TT champions during the golden era of the 60s, and going to the TT has always been my idea of a pilgrimage, a journey I needed to take for the sake of my soul. I'm not sure how Jo felt about 10 days on an island with 10,000 bikes and not a lot of adult supervision, but she readily agreed. Whatever her misgivings, by the time we arrived at the ferry terminal in the city of Liverpool to join the throng heading to the Isle of Man, I could feel that even she was starting to get into the spirit of the adventure.

We arrived early—very early—having been given warning by some old hands about the difficulty of being late. We found ourselves parked at the front of an ever-growing crowd of bikes from Germany, Poland, France and all over the UK, but no one seemed worried by the long wait to board. People walked around and looked at the machines, talked to other riders, sought out information from the TT veterans, read, ate or snoozed behind a wall and out of the wind. Jo read quietly by the bike, but I was too excited for that, in the same innocent way I had been as a child waiting for Christmas.

Eventually, we packed into the fast ferry along with several hundred other bikes, making the journey as comfortable as possible for a couple of poor sailors with some premium pre-booked seats, then rolled off in the Isle of Man capital's, Douglas, into a sea of motorcycles. By the time we got to our hotel, I had gone from simple excitement to grinning like a loon. Our room overlooking Douglas Bay was pleasant, large and full of late afternoon sun. While Jo unpacked and checked emails, I opened a window and lent out to look down the promenade, along the line of hotels and guest houses, and on to the centre of town a few hundred metres away. I knelt on the floor, leaning out of the low window, too excited to do anything useful. The sight amazed me. There were bikes everywhere, parked in every available space, and filled the roads so that pedestrians had to wait minutes for a break in the flow to cross; some said there were 10,000 bikes on the island. We finished unpacking and rushed out into the evening.

Douglas was a pleasant enough sort of place, in the faded style of English seaside resorts of another era. The place had its heyday when holiday travel was made by train and bicycle and flying was a distant dream. It is now cheaper for Britons to fly to the Mediterranean for a beach holiday than to catch the ferry to the Isle of Man, which leaves the island's tourist economy struggling. Fortunately, bikers don't go to Douglas for the ambience. They go for the TT, and as we were about to find out, the TT was much more than a motorcycle race. That year, 2011, was the 100th year of racing on the Isle of Man Mountain Circuit, and it is the 37¾ miles of public roads making up the circuit that have given the TT its character. Modern racing circuits, like Philip Island or Silverstone, are only a few kilometres in length. They are designed for racing and have smooth bitumen surfaces, plenty of corners to keep top speeds down, wide run-off areas on the corners, and are free of obstacles that might injure a fallen rider. The riders practise the perfect line through the corners and try to repeat that for every short lap. A race is generally complete in about 100km, well inside an hour, and on a single tank of fuel.

The TT is nothing like that. The circuit is a closed, public road, with all the shortcomings of any public road. The length of the circuit and its route over Mt Snaefell at 620m means there can be very different weather conditions on different parts of the track. The surface is often poor and always changing, there are no run-off areas, and in many places there are solid obstacles. It is one thing to slide off into the gravel on the corner of a race circuit, quite another to hit a stone wall or a steel bridge pylon. All of this makes the TT extremely dangerous; three riders died during the time we were there.

We watched the racing and practice from different locations each day, as every observation spot had its advantages. Our favourites were a number of churchyards, where ladies auxiliary groups provided home-made morning tea on china plates. The TT is party time on the island, so there was non-racing entertainment and socialising to fill every waking moment. The days flew, and before we had fully settled to the job of enjoying TT week, we had packed and eaten a last Douglas breakfast, done a little more sightseeing and joined a rumbling mass of bikes in the cargo deck of the fast ferry. Soon enough, we were back in the familiar surrounds of Liverpool.

We knew it would take some time for us to fully appreciate the experience we'd had. My simple recounting of our time there does not begin to touch on what it was really all about, what we took away from it and how we felt about returning one day. At first, no matter how we looked at it, the TT was an anachronism, an event left over from another time that had somehow survived, like a hidden valley of dinosaurs. Certainly, it could not be run in the US, Australia, England or almost anywhere else in the developed world. Health and safety concerns aside, so many people having so much fun with so little supervision simply isn't allowed anymore!

Initially, I took the cynical view that the self-governing Isle of Man allowed the event to continue purely for the income it generated each year. But if that had been the extent of our thoughts it would have sold the TT, and all of those who love it, short. The longer we stayed on the island, the more we became aware of and involved with the history of the race. We heard the great stories of the champions who had conquered the mountain, their names being legendary: Mike Hailwood, Giacomo Agostini, Stanley Woods, Joey Dunlop, Phil Read. We heard about Frank Walker, who raced a Royal Enfield in 1914. He was leading when he had a puncture, and after the repair, he fell twice in the chase to get back to the lead. When he crossed the finish line, he overshot the mark, crashed into a barricade and was posthumously awarded third place by the race committee.

Then there is the story of how the Americans brought their Indian motorcycles to the island. These were machines with proper gearboxes and clutches, multicylinder engines and the strength to deal with the immense distances and poor roads of the US, while English bikes of the time were generally belt-driven. The Indians wiped the floor with the local bikes in a 1st, 2nd and 3rd place humiliation, which the locals still make excuses for 100 years later. The winning Indian, ridden by Oliver Godfrey, was so far ahead they made jokes about his lead for years.

Stanley Woods raced on the Isle of Man all his life and had 10 TT victories. He lived on the island, became a successful businessman and lived to the age of 90. Mike Hailwood returned to the TT after 11 years of retirement and rode a 900 Ducati to victory in the 1978 Senior Race, in a feat of riding still talked about in hushed tones. Honda came to the Island for the first time in 1959, with a 125cc racer that took sixth place in the lightweight TT race, at an average speed of 68.29 miles per hour. Honda had started their race team just to compete in the TT, and Hondas dominate the TT races today, with winning average times over 125 miles per hour. Omobona Tenni raced from 1934 and became the first Italian winner in 1937. The stories go on, each a small addition to the legend of the TT.

Even today, new stories are being added, like that of the 2010 crash of Conor Cummins, who fell from his motorcycle at 130 miles per hour, at a part of the circuit called 'the Verandah'. The story of the crash was retold again and again during our eight-day stay. Most of us had seen the helicopter footage of the crash, in our case in 3D, on the big screen at the cinema. Most riders, myself included, would have a sick feeling in the base of their stomachs once they saw smoke pluming from their bike's back wheel, and understood, even before the bike fell, that there was no way back and nowhere to go but over the edge of the mountain. Cummins lived (just), and recovered to ride again in 2011, a modern legend of the TT. A hundred years of these stories mean something very special to those who keep them alive. They mean something to me, at any rate.

The real enigma of the TT, however, lies in the realisation that it celebrates the freedom to choose to do risky things. At a time when our society is increasingly risk-averse, the TT celebrates the folly of its own dangers. Bike riders intuitively understand this. They know what they do is risky and that is part of the attraction. They calculate the risks and accept them willingly as part of the deal. What they hate are attempts to legislate the risks away. For this reason alone, the TT should be preserved and honoured as an antidote to a society that, while it might protect its children from every risk, dooms itself to a future of mediocrity by doing so. The TT reminds us that you can't win without taking risks and that sometimes just to survive is to be a champion.

While our Isle of Man experience had left us buzzing, the remainder of the summer, spent wandering the back-blocks of England and Wales, was a far more relaxed affair. By early November we were back in London. With the first of the cold weather in the air, I spent a few days preparing the bike for storage and hiding it under the shrubbery in our daughter's inner London yard. With the bike well proven, we were ready for the Alps in the spring, as soon as the snow cleared sufficiently.

By the end of winter, we had returned to London with a stock of parts to repair the clutch and a plan for the Alps that involved riding every major pass, starting in the east and working our way west.

The bike was in very good condition when unpacked, and started at first crank—so far so good. A local bike shop, 10 minutes walk away, agreed to fit the parts for the cost of labour and I gave them a list of other work to do so they could still make money from the job. We agreed it was about two to three hours work, and just to show I was organised, I gave the mechanic a print-out from a US Suzuki club website, detailing the job in 41 step-by-step photographs.

When I came back the following day, the mechanic handed me the key and told me it was all done as I wanted and ready to go. Just before I turned the key in the ignition, he said, 'The oil light was on when you brought it in, wasn't it?'

'No, it wasn't.'

'Oh well', he said. 'It must be the sensor then, I'll get one in. You take the bike now and bring it back in two days and I'll fit it.'

I asked him to keep the bike and give it back to me when it was done. Two days passed and I went to the shop to check in.

The bike was not ready. The sensor had been replaced and there was still no oil pressure. I left them to solve the problem and phoned the next day. 'Umm', the mechanic began, 'it seems, well, we left out the oil pump drive gear when we assembled the engine. It is still attached to the old clutch basket, which you took with you. Do you still have it?' Fortunately I did. I took it around to the shop, leaving it without comment. Another day passed before I called again to see if the bike was ready. There was a new problem, this time an oil leak. They needed some special gasket stuff. I went to the workshop to see what was going on. The oil leak was from a crack in the crankcase at the point where the oil sensor screwed in.

The following day, I went back. The crack had widened (over-tightening a tapered thread will do that every time), the special gasket stuff hadn't worked, and the mechanic looked sheepish. The shop manager was all apologies. 'We will have to get the crack welded up by a specialist welder', he told me.

'Please do', I said, and walked out bike-less once again.

Three days later, the manager rang. The bike had been ridden back from the welders and was fine. I hurried around to see it. It was on the stand and the belly pan was still to be fitted. The side of the crank case where the oil pressure sensor had been, however, looked a little strange. To start, the sensor was gone, but the whole casting lug that had held the sensor had melted away and blended into the front section of the crank case. It looked a little like a Salvador Dali melted clock—a Dali Suzuki!

Back at the house, having cooled my temper somewhat, I composed a polite letter explaining what remedy I sought and arranged for the letter to be delivered by hand. But I was far too frustrated and angry to sit around in London and wait for a solution. Jo and I borrowed a couple of backpacks from our daughter and son-in-law, threw together some of our motorcycle gear and a few borrowed items, including maps, and caught the train to the city of Winchester. From there, we started to hike the South Downs Way. A day later, I phoned the bike shop. The manager had received my letter. He said he understood exactly what my lawyer would do to their little business with the rough end of a pineapple if the bike wasn't returned to a proper state.

A week later, we were back in London, footsore but pleased to have hiked about 60 miles of bucolic English countryside and finally over the worst of my rage. I rang the shop. They had sourced a second-hand engine of the correct type and similar age and fitted it. It was 'running perfect'. I walked to the shop, where the manager handed me the keys, said nothing and shrugged. I shrugged in response, climbed on and rode away.

The next morning, we packed the luggage and rolled out of London, headed for the Midlands for a test run. The bike was, indeed, 'running perfect', so after 1000 miles and three days of testing, we rode into the Channel port of Harwich and put the bike and ourselves on an overnight ferry to the Hook of Holland. We had lost a precious month, some money and a little of our store of patience, but we had nothing to complain about. We were in good health, we had a reliable bike and the freedom to go where we liked. At last our Alps adventure could get underway.

'Where to first?' asked Jo.

'I've always wanted to go to Pilsen in the Czech Republic.'

Jo gave me that quizzical look of hers.

'That's where they invented Pilsener', I continued. 'It's important we check and see how it's going.'

'Someone has to', she said dryly.

Three days later, we were across Germany and lining up with the other English speakers for the brewery tour, quite interested in the workings of a super modern plant, now owned by a huge multinational brewing company, but more interested in getting to the cellars for the tasting. It was a blistering hot day outside, but 5 degrees in the cellars, and we were chilled to the bone by the time we had assured ourselves that the beer was, as we hoped, fit for human consumption, if not the artisanal product it had once been. The town of Pilsen itself was also a pleasant surprise, a little shabby and run-down, but comfortable, liveable and affordable, the sort of place where you can sit in a café watching the world go by, a glass of the local beverage in your hand, and not feel like you want to be somewhere else. Which was unfortunate in a way, because we did need to be somewhere else—we had to be in the Alps while there was summer enough to do it. We took the back roads south out of Pilsen, stopped just short of the Austrian border, and used the last of our local currency on coffee and cake before pushing on again over the mountains.

We picked up the pace over some almost deserted mountain roads and Jo asked me how I felt about the new bike now that we had some miles up.

'I like it', I said. 'There are no frills, but it's strong and sure-footed, and seems to do everything well enough.'

'Plain Suzie then?' said Jo.

'Not Suzie, that's too fancy. Maybe Sue.'

'Just Sue?' said Jo.

'Why not? Just Sue it is.'

I pulled out past a small car on a steep pinch and opened the throttle. Just Sue shook her head, settled her back end, and let out a satisfied roar. Within a few seconds, the small car had disappeared from our mirrors, and Just Sue was over the crest and flying south.

All of this messing about finally got us to Slovenia, then to the Italian city of Trieste, perched at the top of the Adriatic and attached to Italy by the slimmest of land bridges. Trieste is not in the Alps, but we needed to start somewhere, and it had such a romantic name we couldn't help but go there. To the north, the Julian Alps in western Slovenia rose rapidly into the main range, but on a balmy day in Trieste it was the city itself that focused our attention. It was a place that had somehow been suspended in time. At first glance, nothing was happening there, and nothing seemed to have happened for a long time.

With Just Sue parked securely under our apartment, we got out to explore the city on foot. Trieste, we knew, had an interesting history, well worth the visit, because later it would give us insights into the nature of the Italian interest in the Alps, and the Alps' interest in Italy. Trieste had been a sleepy Adriatic fishing village for hundreds of years until an emerging Austro-Hungarian Empire, keen to establish a substantial seaport and a link to the world, prodded it to life. The port flourished and the city grew until, World War I, it looked much as it does today. It had an inner-city core of Italian traders (mainly Venetian) and a Slavic outer city drawn from the hinterland it serviced. The ports were busy, the town was prosperous, and it had the multicultural allure of great port cities everywhere.

The war changed all of that. When the new and ascendant nation states divided the spoils of the collapsed Austro-Hungarian Empire at the conclusion of hostilities, Trieste somehow became Italian. Whatever the sense of it, the Italian army marched into the city unopposed, and claimed it for Italy. The city's port activities ceased abruptly with its change of management, as the Italians didn't need a port on the eastern side of the Adriatic tenuously connected to its markets, already possessing well-established facilities at Venice. Nor was Italian hegemony widely applauded at the time. US President Woodrow Wilson was said to be furious about the arrangement; the Americans had insisted on principles for post-war restructuring, including that national boundaries should reflect traditional cultural and ethnic divisions, rather than the political proclivities of the winners. Even with its few thousand Italian traders, Trieste could never have been called an Italian city. But the deal was done long before the Americans entered the war, by governments firmly anchored in the traditions of the 19th century.

Trieste didn't die, but neither did it progress, and much of its old elegance remains. Some of it is well hidden, while others parts are nicely restored for the tourist trade. We booked into a pension in what had once been a palatial villa. It had a substantial façade covering a confusing maze of shoddily-built passages and doors, which had us planning our way out in case of fire. It was comfortable, though, and its ramshackle feel set the scene for our visit. The tourist centre of the town was nicely presented, as these places usually are, but the waterfront docklands were empty and unused and appeared to have been that way for a long time. There was simply no economy to justify redevelopment.

There were, however, plenty of reminders of Italian efforts to reinforce its legitimacy in its newly acquired lands. The worst of these had been built during the long period of Fascist rule, when Italian nationalism must have driven a thriving economy of sculptors. On a hill overlooking the city, a huge plinth supported a cluster of super-sized figures with grotesquely overdeveloped physiques, busy hoisting the Italian flag. Far more appealing was a set of life-sized bronze figures by the waterfront. One was an Italian soldier, perhaps a marine, wading ashore with the Italian flag flying. I liked the fact that the figure was life-sized and looked like the sort of wiry peasant who would have done the fighting, but in fact there had been no heroic storming of Trieste. The other bronzes depicted two handsome women sewing the Italian flag. The detail was beautifully rendered and they seemed elegant and, almost appropriate. Our final perplexing discovery in Trieste was a museum. Going through the tourist brochures (the fine print, mind you), we discovered that there was Museum of the Risorgimento. The Risorgimento (literally 'Resurgence') is the name given to the 19th century movement to establish a united Italian state. Its central achievement was the amalgamation of Sicilian-controlled southern Italy into the federation in the 1860s, championed by the durable Italian hero Garibaldi. This seemed to have little to do with Trieste a half-century later, so being the curious types we are, we set out to see for ourselves what such a museum might contain.

The Museum of the Risorgimento took a little finding. It was only marked on one map and was very poorly signposted. We had nearly given up and gone to look for coffee and gelato when Jo found a portico sealed off with a metal grille. Next to the door were two small signs, easily missed, that announced the museum and made clear that it would only be open two mornings a week. This was not one of those mornings. The place looked dirty and uncared for, and we doubted it would have many visitors, so we walked back to the harbour, bought some fabulous gelato and let the museum drift from our consciousness. We could only guess at what the Museum of the Risorgimento displayed. Perhaps it was a balanced and thoughtful presentation on the achievements of Italian Nationalism. Whatever its message, however, few in modern Trieste would ever hear it.

The great travel writer Jan Morris described Trieste as a city 'out of time', a city that is 'nowhere'.[2] It certainly had a whiff of musty melancholy about it, the sort of scent I associate with the bosom of a great aunt—lavender soap and disappointment. We still had the whole of the Alps in front of us and already there were questions and stories demanding our attention.

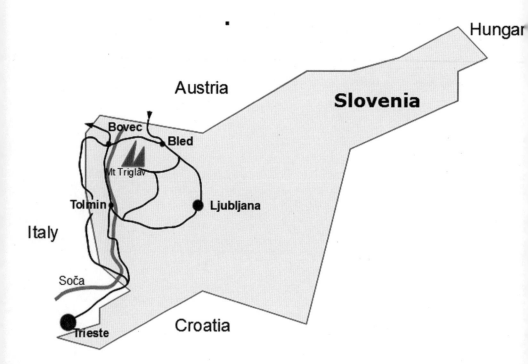

3

THE JULIAN ALPS AND THE DESERT FOX

The weather was still hot when we left Trieste, clambering up onto the escarpment to the north. In that sort of heat, we would normally wear riding suits with large mesh panels, which allow the air to circulate and keep the level of sweaty misery under control. But on a journey such as ours, we could only pack one riding suit each (the ones we were wearing), and they needed to be suitable for the high mountains and cold weather of the Alps. In theory, we would just put up with the few hot days, but this summer the hot days stretched into weeks and we suffered badly.

We could, of course, have done what many do and ride in lighter clothing, but having spent a lifetime preaching the importance of always wearing good protective gear on a bike, I wasn't likely to change because of a little discomfort. You can never predict when a bike is likely to go down and any fall without protective clothing would be a bad one. Our best solution was to start early and finish early, before the worst of the heat, breaking up the riding with plenty of stops.

We planned our route north along the line of the Italian–Slovenian border, finally dropping down into the Soča Valley on the Slovenian side, over the Passo di Tanamea. Our targets were the valley towns of Bovec and Kobarid, which would act as our base for an exploration of the Julijske Alpe, or 'Julian Alps'. The traffic was light, the coffee stops regular, and the ride an easy sweep though comparatively gentle mountain passes. Above 1000m altitude, the late morning temperature was pleasant, but by lunch we had dropped down into the breathless heat of the valley and were more than ready to call it a day.

The decision to base ourselves in the valley was a good one, as its towns were comfortable, well serviced and provided easy access to the mountains. But the history of the valley also gave us some clues to the Italian Alpine experience, which we might have missed if we had been based in the popular tourist area around Bled, or the capital Ljubljana. It was in this area, roughly along the line of the Soča River, that titanic battles for control of the Alps had taken place, in a conflict to rival the more famous battles of the Somme in northern France for intensity and brutality.

Stark reminders of the struggle for control of the Alps were everywhere in the valley, recorded in memorials large and small, the decaying ruins of fortifications and the small, barely marked graveyards scattered across the mountains. Some of these were achingly sad. We stopped for coffee just north of Triglav Dom

(1618m) and beside the roughed-out car park, there were three tiny graves, marked with stones and crude crosses made from strips of iron riveted together. These were the graves of three Russian prisoners who had died making the road, of cold or disease or avalanche, a long, long way from home. What was less clear from those early discoveries was the reason the fighting took place there at all. An answer to this more interesting question started to coalesce a few days later, when we followed a winding mountain track north from the town of Tolmin, located an hour's ride south down the valley.

The road wound up to the north of the town, turned to gravel and narrowed to a single car width. Occasional wider ledges allowed for passing with a little backing and filling. The roads themselves have never bothered us on a bike, representing a kind of passive risk. It is neutral in that it is the same for everyone, and there is no point in fighting it or cursing it or getting frustrated with it. A good rider adjusts to the road and stays safe. What does bother us, however, are other road users— the ones who come around blind corners so fast they cannot stop on the gravel surface and hit an oncoming bike sending it off the edge and into the abyss. When this is a risk, I compensate as far as I can by reducing our speed, using the horn and always looking for the 'way out' if the worst happens. This was one of those painfully slow and nervous rides.

The road broke out onto a low pass, then stopped. We parked the bike at the start of a walking track and began a 20 minute climb through a light forest. When we finally emerged into a rising meadow, we were amazed to see an elegant wooden building above us. We had found the Memorial Church of the Holy Spirit, built in 1916 by members of the Austrian 3rd

Mountain Brigade. The building had been designed by Viennese artist Remigius Geyling, who was then a first lieutenant. We had seen many war memorials in many countries, but few would match this simple, wooden building for restrained beauty. The building was perfectly proportioned and exquisitely decorated in blue, with gold highlighting. It had a commanding view down through a high mountain valley. Surrounded by majestic peaks, the view of the chapel from below gave the building a human perspective, and made the climb entirely worth the effort. Inside, the light was subdued with a gentle shafts radiating from high windows. The inside walls might easily cause a jaded traveller to stop in sombre reflection, being covered with the names of 2,564 Austrian soldiers, carefully lettered in black on larch panels.

We stopped in the chapel for a long time, partly to steel ourselves for the walk back to the bike, but mainly to enjoy the space. We read and pronounced the German names and touched them with our fingers, and stood alone at the door, letting the serenity of the place wash over us. After a while, a man came in from the back of the building and we struck up a conversation. He was a local teacher and amateur historian who worked for the tourist commission during the long summer break. His knowledge of the local military history was comprehensive but, more importantly, nuanced. Within a few minutes of conversation, he had challenged many of the conceptions I had formed from my research.

'That isn't right', he told me. 'The Italians were not poorly equipped. Their equipment was generally better than the Austrians ... No, those figures are wrong. The casualties were much lower. The Italians wanted to maximise the impact of their sacrifice to the other Allies. Most historians just accepted the official figures ... You're right, the number of deserters was high. We don't know how many, but their number is probably included in the official dead ... The Italians didn't send food parcels to their soldiers held prisoner by the Austrians, to discourage surrender. Many prisoners died from hunger and cold as a result ... No, we don't know how many ... That is true, but there was bad generalship on both sides.'

There was much more like this, all of it thought-provoking. We said our farewell, took a few photos and started back, feeling that we at last had a focus for this part of our journey.

In the Soča, we started to find a more subtle view of the events that shaped this part of the Alps 100 years ago, and in particular the way the trauma of the two World Wars and a Cold War shaped national boundaries and national characters. When studied through the filter of these recent conflicts, modern Slovenia seems like a lucky place. Lacking the strategic assets of location, land mass, population and resources, the Slovenes have been able to establish their independence and put together a viable mini-state, in charge of its own destiny. They have achieved this despite having a reasonably diverse ethnic mix and lacking the sort of tribalism that sometimes marks successful mini-states. History hasn't dealt nearly such good cards to dozens of other small groups seeking independence.

Until 1991, Slovenia had been part of larger empires and states. The Roman, Holy Roman and then Austro-Hungarian empires all took their turn at control, until the Austro-Hungarian collapse at the end of WWI. At that time, the Italians gained control of a western slice of the country, including the Soča Valley, and the remainder threw in their lot with the short-lived State of Slovenes, Croats and Serbs. A month after it was formed, the new state was absorbed into the Kingdom of Serbs, Croats and Slovenes, where it remained until being ceded to Tito's Socialist Federal Republic of Yugoslavia after World War II. With the breakup of the Soviet bloc in 1991, the Slovenes saw their chance and established their independence, taking with them about one per cent of Yugoslavia's population and about 15 per cent of its industry.

Along the Soča Valley, there was plenty of evidence of the struggle waged by Italy for control of this easternmost part of the Alps, but it took many more weeks of travel and a much better understanding of modern Italy before we had an explanation for why the Italians had gone there at all. In the meantime, we rode a long loop around the Julian Alps, over a couple of short hot days. The Julian Alps are lower, less spectacular and, as a result, less well known than those in Switzerland, but they were nonetheless a great place for us to explore and an easy start before we tackled the tougher mountains in the west.

Most of the Julian Alps fall into the Triglav National Park. Unsurprisingly for a country as small as Slovenia, this is its only national park, and forms a substantial part of the landmass. It is said that from the top of Mount Triglav (elevation 2864m) in the centre of the park, you can see the whole of Slovenia on a clear day, and perhaps this is so—we could certainly see the cloud-shrouded mountain from a good part of Slovenia! The upside of this is that the roads are well maintained and the park is spotlessly clean and well used. The downside is that it is always busy with tourists and there is a lot of traffic on the main routes.

In the east, where the park and the mountains taper out and roll down onto the plains towards Ljubljana, the country is less spectacular, the tourists few and the traffic light. We had an easy day through these eastern hills, stopping for a picnic lunch in the high country and a roadside coffee at a little shop by a mountain stream. It was about then that we decided there was a lot to like about Slovenia. To start with, the place was spotless, but Ljubljana was also a handy size, large enough to support a good cultural life but small enough to be liveable, and the countryside was close by and accessible to all. It was a place where everything worked and you didn't need to be a rocket scientist to buy a bus ticket.

After several weeks of relentless hot weather, we were happy to spend a few extra days in Kobarid, hoping that a cool change would sweep through. We put on our hiking boots (which strangely look just the same as our riding boots) and set off on a walk through the district on a well-marked trail. The circuit took us via ruins from the early Middle Ages, World War I defensive works, and an easy ramble along the beautiful river. It also led us to the Italian Charnal House, located on a hill overlooking the town. This memorial was built around the 14th century Church of St Anthony, which is does nothing to enhance. It was constructed by the Fascist government of Mussolini as part of the same nation-building program that had produced the over-blown monument we had seen in Trieste. It certainly gave the same impression of pompous self-importance. Benito Mussolini himself had opened the memorial in 1938. It was a stark counterpoint to the simple and isolated chapel above Tolmin. Still, we walked around each gallery and read the names of the Giovannis and Luigis, and found the surname Longo, the family name of an old friend. The site contains the remains of 7,014 Italian soldiers, both known and unknown.

Back in the town, our final stop was the Kobariški Muzej,

tucked into a nicely renovated building near the centre and dedicated to the events of World War I. Like all of these things in Slovenia, the museum was well run and well presented, and good value for the entrance fee. It had a small collection of artefacts, but nothing of great importance. What it did have that made it accessible to the wider public, and not just military history types, was a stunning collection of photographs. Appropriately mounted and well lit, the period detail they contained was fascinating. They captured the intensity of surgeons conducting an operation in the open air, the radiant smiles of village girls standing on the stairs, the wizened grins of wiry little men who had fought this bitter mountain war, and provided a link to the real people of an exceptional time. We were left with the impression that this newly independent country had managed a good balance in the way they approached their own troubled history. Mature and respectful were the words that came to my mind.

So, how did the Italians, whose whole history had been hammered out down on the peninsula, end up in the Alps? The answer to this question lies somewhere in the middle of the 19th century. This was a time when England, France and others were nascent states, when the United States was marching westwards across that continent, and even the 70-year-old colonies of Australia had started the inevitable march to a federation. In contrast, Italy remained an unruly alliance of various regions, with little sense of national identity and a past rooted in family and region. The Risorgimento brought together cities and provinces with no unifying sense of what it meant to be Italian. The solution seemed to lie with military adventure. After all, the great European powers had powerful armies or navies, which they used to capture and maintain empires across the globe. It was logical that the new Italy should do the same.

A large army and navy were established (larger than a poor country like Italy could afford) and adventures were launched in an attempt to feed the desire for Italian success against a significant European foe. In 1866, the Italians launched an attack against Austria at Custoza and, despite a significant numerical advantage, managed to turn this into a disastrous defeat thanks to the inspired incompetence of the Italian generals, Alfonso Ferrero la Marmora and Enrico Cialdini. In the same year, the new and well-equipped Italian navy managed to orchestrate a defeat at the hands of a numerically inferior Austrian fleet in the Adriatic, near the island of Lissa. The battle is notable as the first between ironclads and the last to involve ships directly ramming the enemy. Historians have blamed the defeat, once again, on poor generalship and the squabbling of the many 'admirals'. Officially, these catastrophes were portrayed as victories, but there was no hiding the reality that the new nation of Italy had been humiliated.

Other adventures in North Africa followed, none of them successful, but all sold to the public as great victories for the nation. It is difficult to overstate the Italian appetite for military adventure in the late 19th century. Italy, and many Italians, did not wish to be seen by the other European states as the fifth wheel on the wagon, to use Bismark's expression, and found the condescension of the French English and Germans humiliating. Having proven too weak to seek military success in continental Europe, the Italian hawks became determined to establish colonies elsewhere, which would prove the country's power and produce the riches the state needed.

The most bellicose and influential of Italian politicians was Francesco Crispi, who, according to the historian David Gilmour, 'was eager to quarrel—and if possible fight wars—with almost everyone (especially the French)'.[3] Under Crispi's prime ministership, the Italians pursued their ambitions in Ethiopia, Eritrea and Somalia. Unfortunately, his claim that the native 'barbarians' understood nothing but the power of guns turned out to be true. The tribesmen rallied against the Italians, inflicting some notable defeats, and restricted Italian occupation to a few coastal cities. This was hardly the grand and profitable colonial enterprise the Italian hawks had in mind, but despite the lack of success, or perhaps because of it, monuments were built to false heroes, and streets were renamed to glorify the incompetent.

All countries fabricate a history to suit their needs, but on this ancient peninsula, the need was expressed differently. The Italian nationalists were caught between the martial legend of their Roman forebears and the military strength of their European peers. They were desperate for a real victory, a national victory, not against ancient tribal warriors in Africa (although even there, a little victory or two would have been useful to defuse anxiety), but against a European power. It was a dangerous obsession that would cost the people of Italy and Austria dearly.

If World War I was an inevitability for much of Europe, it was not entirely so for Italy. At the outbreak of hostilities, Italy had been part of the Triple Alliance with Austria and Germany for 60 years, an arrangement that required Italy to renounce any territorial ambition in the north and so provide Austria with a secure southern flank. It also gave Italy a good reason to sit out the fighting. But all countries have their reasons to go to war.

The new nations of Canada and Australia threw their youthful enthusiasm, not to mention their youth, into a European war, in an effort to demonstrate that they too had joined the nations of the world and, importantly, because their national interests were tied to the Empire. Even the sleeping giant of America eventually found reason to spend its blood and gold.

David Gilmour describes the Italian mood succinctly:

'Although the Italians had no foes, except those they chose to make ... they had not stopped dreaming of military triumph against someone. The defeats at Custoza and Lissa still rankled and, in the minds of many, still required a baptism of fire to avenge them. ... [T]hey would be fighting so that they could consider themselves—and be considered by others—as a martial nation.'[4]

Once the war had started, Italy began to negotiate with its Triple Alliance partners, but also, importantly, with the Triple Entente countries, Britain, Russia and France. The negotiations went slowly while the Italians played for time to see which side would emerge with the upper hand. In the end, however, the Triple Entente could afford to be more generous. After all, it was not its citizens whom it was bargaining away. A deal was struck to allow Italy control of the Alps to the watershed, and to push its boundary east around the Adriatic, in return for the Italians opening up a southern flank against the Austrians. Finally, Italy had its grand European war.

Despite the boasts of the Italian commander and principal hawk General Luigi Cardona that his army would sweep into Vienna within weeks, the Italians found themselves bogged down on the Izonzo Front, along the Soča River. Cardona continued to launch poorly-planned and ill-prepared offensives until 1917, when the Germans sent some extra divisions south, to give the Austrian command the power they needed for a counter-offensive. The Germans brought new techniques and thinking from the Western Front with them and drove the Italian Army back to the River Piave, just north of Venice, in a smashing blow know as the Battle of Caporetto.

Erwin Rommel was a young German officer who fought on the Izonzo Front and later rose to the rank of Field Marshall during World War II. He earned the appellation 'The Desert Fox' for his exploits leading German and, interestingly, Italian troops in North Africa. Rommel, though a loyal officer during World War II, was well regarded by Allied forces as a professional soldier, who ignored orders to kill Jewish prisoners, civilians and commandos, and was party to the attempted assassination of Hitler. His exploits on the Izonzo Front, however, did much to shape his later skill as a commander and earned him decorations for bravery and leadership. After the World War I, he wrote extensively on the small groups tactics developed during the campaign. In an unexpected connection with this part of the world, I had read his book on the Izonzo campaign as a young National Serviceman, more than 40 years before, and *Infantry Tactics* is still considered to be important professional reading, 60 years after it was written. The final sad sidebar on The Desert Fox is that when the attempt on Hitler's life failed, he agreed to commit suicide in return for Hitler's guarantee that his family would be safe.

The Battle of Caporetto had at least one good outcome for the Italians. Cordona, who was allied to and protected by the vacillating and ineffective king, was finally sacked on the insistence of the British and French, who were forced to send divisions to reinforce the front. A new commander stabilised the front and refused to waste further Italian lives in ill-prepared offensives. The German divisions returned to the north, the war eventually petered out and the Austro-Hungarian Empire collapsed. Italy had lost 14,000 square kilometres of its territory and over a million of its citizens, but had managed to pick the winning side. The Italian Army marched unopposed into Trieste and took the heights above the Soča River without firing a shot.

All of this was presented to the Italian public as a great victory, but the country plunged into turmoil. From the chaos, an opportunistic newspaper editor named Benito Mussolini emerged to create the first Fascist government, and started building some very ugly monuments.

By the time the story of the Italians in the eastern Alps had coalesced for us, out of the hills around Bovec, the weather had changed and low, dark clouds filled the tops of the mountain valleys. We asked some locals if it would rain. 'Maybe this afternoon,' they said, 'but in the mountains, now.' It is best not to ride the mountains in the rain, and best not to ignore the advice of locals, but we were buoyed by the cooler weather so decided to pack and move on. By late morning, we were climbing out of Bovec to the north and into Passo del Predil. There was a little rain, but the road had plenty of grip, and we hurried on into the delicious cool. Beyond the mountains lay Italy, more passes, and then Austria, and a different view of the Alps entirely.

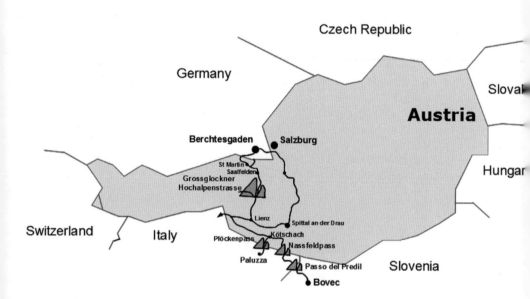

4

GROSSGLOCKNER HOCHALPENSTRASSE

We were just starting to feel comfortable on our ride up into Passo del Predil when the weather closed in, and the folly of ignoring local advice became obvious, as it usually does. By the time we reached the pass, with its monuments and signage, our conversation over the bike's intercom had dried up and I wasn't in the humour for stopping. We plunged over the edge onto the rainy side of the hill and started to feel the full force of the storm. The road was too narrow to stop, so we pushed on to find a place where we could put on our wet weather suits. By the time we had found a park and suited up, it was too late. We were already soaked and it wasn't hard to tell that Jo was mighty cross we hadn't stopped to suit up before the rain hit.

Deciding when to put on the rubber suits always requires a bit of judgement. If you put them on too early, the heat builds up, leaving you soaked through with condensation and sweat. If you leave it too late, the suit goes on over wet clothing and you can never get comfortable after that. Jo always tends towards an early suit up, while I leave it as long as possible because—well, just because. This day, I had misjudged things badly and we were wet and miserable an hour into our ride. As always when things like this happen, I felt bad about screwing up, and I was thankful when Jo decided to keep her thoughts to herself.

Miserable or not, we hustled Just Sue on, taking care on the wet roads but intent on covering enough distance to make the day worthwhile. On the Italian side of the mountain, the weather settled into the steady rain of a bleak and cold day. We worried away at the back roads to the north, then west, and on to the town of Pontebba, providing access to Nassfeldpass and Austria. Although low at only 1,552m, the pass provided both a good riding road and a tourist road with enough interest to keep our minds off our clammy backsides. We ended the day, still in our rain gear, at a warm B&B in the town of Kötschach and managed to find a comforting meal and a therapeutic red wine at a local pub. It had been a good day's work after an inauspicious start.

The next morning over breakfast, our landlady surprised us by introducing her Australian son-in-law. She had noticed that Jo was travelling on an Australian passport and not many Aussies made it to this nice little town. Peter had been a police officer, but had moved to his Austrian-born wife's hometown with their two children. He didn't get much chance to chat with native English speakers and was keen to talk. For our part, we were pleased to get a little insider information on the district and hear the interesting story that had brought him to that place. Our plan at that stage was to head west, then north towards the German Alps, but by the time we said our farewell and loaded up Just Sue we had decided to make a detour. On Peter's advice, we rode straight south and climbed into the Plöckenpass a few kilometres outside the town. The road rose steeply through a series of sweeping bends, only spoiled by the indifferent surface. With clear, cold weather in the mountains, it was an exhilarating ride up through the pine forests, through long, open-sided tunnels where Just Sue's V-twin boomed off the walls, and out into an open pass at 1,362m altitude. We plunged down the Italian side, only to turn around at the little village of Paluzza, and ride back through and into Austria again. Although it is only a low pass, the Plöcken climbs through dramatic switchbacks towards the Austrian border. By the time we were back at our starting point just outside Kötschach, the weather was looking fine and our spirits were high. There is nothing like an early morning ride through the mountains to start the day.

The weather stayed fine as we zigged west towards Sillian, then zagged east to Spittal an der Drau. It was at about this point that we realised our track over the map was starting to look like the scrawling of a child. We were determined to experience as many of the great alpine bike roads as we could and there was no neat way to do that. Our navigation consisted of marking off the roads that mattered, then linking them up in the best way possible. Some backtracking was inevitable, but Jo was spending a great deal of time trying to inject some efficiency into our route.

There is a huge motorway running through Spittal, the one

we had used a few weeks earlier when transiting to Slovenia. For our leg north, we stayed off the motorway and took the old road sweeping up through the Lieser River Valley. The road seemed to race north as fast as the river ran south, with an excellent surface and open corners. It was the sort of road that bike riders in other countries travelled days to find, while here it was unexceptional. What made it memorable for us, however, was the way it shadowed the new motorway up the valley, crossing back and forth under the massive concrete structure and providing a surprisingly grand view as we exited many corners.

It almost goes without saying that the weather had turned cranky by the time we reached the town of Hallein, crossed into Germany, and settled for the night at Berchtesgaden. The Alps are self-evidently only a small part of Germany, and not where the character of the nation was formed. That drama had been played out on the plains of central Germany, which is an area with no defensible borders and historically hostile tribes on every side. The Alps have, however, still been important in the country's history and culture, Germans having keenly felt the allure of the mountains.

Adolf Hitler was fascinated by the Alps, particularly the area around Berchtesgaden. During the 1930s, the ruling Nazi Party used the Alps extensively in propaganda films and images. The Alps provided an arena in which the mettle of the Aryan race could be tested and glorified. Films about the Alps and the lives of the people there, who were presented as strong, independent, upright folk (Nazi code for white, Aryan and pure), became popular in Germany during the 1920s and 1930s. It was a time when alpine heroes—German ones at least—were lauded in the press and rewarded for their bravery with a handshake from the Führer. Austrian-born Hitler had an enduring fascination with the mountains, visiting Berchtesgaden many times in the 1920s, and is reputed to have written the second volume of *Mein Kampf* while staying at a Berchtesgaden Hotel.

For much of the 19th century, mountain climbing had largely been the province of English climbers. By the Great Depression, however, Continental climbers were proving themselves in the most difficult ascents. For some who had been too young to participate in World War I, it was their chance to undertake a dangerous endeavour and test their bravery. In 1925, a Munich climber named Willy Welzenbach devised a system to assess the difficulty of climbs, and within a year Mussolini had started to issue medals for the most difficult grade, the sixth. By the middle of the 1930s, there was an unannounced competition to conquer the few great climbs that remained.

Many of these last climbs were on the north face of the mountains, where lack of sun and exposure to the weather made life hard for climbers. The north face of the Eiger is the most famous example, and the subject of several films, including the gripping German film *The North Face* (2008). The race to be first to the top claimed many lives, but those who survived and succeeded were lauded as national Aryan heroes. By the mid-1930s, the Alps had been politicised, and the sport of climbing had shifted from the gentlemanly pursuit of wealthy amateurs to the technical business of professionals, undertaken for national prestige. Hitler was a strong believer in this alpine competition and actively supported German climbers even before he came to power.

Hitler later bought his own villa, just above the town of Berchtesgaden. Over the following 15 years, until it was bombed to rubble towards the end of World War II, he spent about six months of each year there. The villa was expanded to become a second seat of government away from Berlin, and cute alpine houses were built nearby by most of the Nazi hierarchy. Known as the Berghof, the fortified complex eventually covered more than 32 square kilometres. This is where British Prime Minister Neville Chamberlain came to meet Hitler, and where he agreed to German occupation of the Sudetenland area of Czechoslovakia, in the final events leading up to the World War. It is where the Duke and Duchess of Windsor (aka, the abdicated King Edward VII of the United Kingdom and his American wife, Wallis Simpson) came to visit Hitler, which, unsurprisingly, fuelled rumours that the couple were Nazi sympathisers. Hitler is reported to have commented later that he thought Wallis would have made a good queen.

This fascination with the mountains is easily understood through the prism of our 21st century sensibilities, and it seems unsurprising that Hitler, or anyone, would find the mountains inspiring. We would discover later in our journey that this was not always the case, and that the Alps have not always been seen in the positive light by which we view them today. Throughout most of history, in fact, mountains were places of monsters and dragons, unknown dangers and hostile tribes. At the simplest level, the mountains inspired fear. The mountains were dangerous places, where the terrain, wolves and unpredictable weather could kill the unwary, but the fear was also deeply rooted in superstition and religion. Although the valley meadows had been farmed for millennia, and many of the passes were in use more than 3,000 years ago, few ever ventured into the high mountains, and fewer still would have climbed one just because they could. To the medieval mind, they were simply ugly.

In the Dark and Middle Ages, devils were real, and sorcery had power over the lives of poor and rich alike. Stories of giants, beasts and belligerent gods were ever-present at this time, but it was the nature of the mountains—their inaccessibility and emptiness—that concentrated such legends in the popular imagination. Every valley had its own tales and superstitions, no doubt told and retold around the fire through interminably long winters. My favourite story, in which an enterprising fellow trades his soul to the devil in return for supernatural power, originates in the French Alps. As he grew old and closer to payback time, he went to see the Pope to ask for forgiveness. The Pope, who obviously wasn't in on the joke, granted forgiveness on the condition that the man heard mass in Rome, Milan and his home village of Bessans in the same day. The scoundrel used his supernatural powers to do the rounds in the specified time and cheated both the Pope and the devil. I love these stories because the spirits and demons involved are often mortally fallible and imbued with human vices and virtues.

At a practical level, the mountains were a useful place to locate all of the sources of evil, simply because the land itself was of no practical use. The soils were poor and they provided little opportunity for farming, grazing was limited to some lower slopes and then only in the short summer and for hunters, armed with spears, bows and dogs, they were just plain hard work. There was nothing attractive about them at all. Of course, this kind of thinking wasn't limited to those less sophisticated times. As late as my own childhood in the 1950s, swamps, marshlands and mangroves were seen as an ugly blight on the countryside, only useful once drained or developed, or as rubbish dumps. Now there are boardwalks through the mangroves near where we live so that we can appreciate this important ecosystem.

By the 20th century, an innate fear of the mountains had largely been turned into a positive, but equally unrealistic view. By the time of Hitler's rise to power, the novel *Heidi* by Johanna Spyri had painted a picture of the Alps as wholesome and healthy. The syrupy novel has been filmed many times, including a 1937 Hollywood production with painted backdrops and Shirley Temple playing the eponymous Heidi. Nearly 100 years after the book's publication, Julie Andrews made the hills come alive with the sound of music and cemented the romance of the Alps for the 20th century.

These days, the town of Berchtesgaden is a touristy village, with hotels clustered around a raging stream though the centre. There is a museum where the Berghof guesthouse stood, which we were assured was very good, but we didn't go. I had been to enough war sites that week already. Instead, we walked across to the railway station, which was, the same good source had told us, build by the Nazi architect Albert Speer. We walked through it and looked at it from several angles before deciding that Albert must have had a bad day, then diverted our sightseeing to a nearby supermarket, bought some food and wine and adjourned to our hotel room where we could watch the raging stream and enjoy the peace of the evening.

In an earlier life, Jo had been a teacher at a high school in the Australian capital city of Canberra, where she met Indu, a fellow science teacher, and her husband Gerhard, who had become our friends. We knew that Gerhard's family had a cabin in the mountains south of Berchtesgaden, just over the border in Austria, and that they spent some time there each summer. We had a few other scraps of information from postcards and conversations, but no real idea where it was. Jo decided that we should find the cabin: we had found Scovorodino in Russia, she pointed out, so how hard could it be? I recalled the long and wet search we had made in 2008 for that Siberian town, which, despite its 10,000 inhabitants, managed to evade us for some time.

We had a rough idea of the district from our maps, and a simple triangulation from the information we had led us to the area northeast of the towns of St Martin and Weissbach. This was at least a start. We stopped in the town of St Martin and started our search. At first we found little to encourage us, but then, up a narrow road at a place where walkers could park their cars and set out into the hills, we found a map—not just any map, but a blow-up of a 1:25,000 topographic survey map, of sufficiently large scale that it showed every building and every fence junction. It was the sort of map with which an old soldier could feel at home!

Studying it closely, we found a lone building, high in the mountains close to the frontier. It was worth a shot. I drew a mud map in my notebook, carefully listing each junction and fence gate, and off we went, climbing from the village of Weissbach up a narrow goat-track of a road, stopping occasionally to check our notes but mainly following our compass. After half-an-hour's ascent, we rounded a corner and saw a small cottage, sitting alone on the edge of a clearing. It was certainly the cottage shown on the map, but was it the cabin we sought? A little further around the next bend, an old gasthous marked the border, and was still doing a slow trade for walkers heading into the hills. On a cold, wet day, customers were scarce, so we ordered hot chocolate and struck up a conversation with the proprietor. We asked if she knew our friends, and she confirmed she did, very well. The cabin was just back a few hundred yards—the very one we saw—and they had, she said, been there just a few days before. We left a note at the bar and got Just Sue moving again, on a road so greasy it was difficult not to spin the back wheel, and I had trouble finding a place firm enough to park when we reached the cabin.

The place was empty and we carefully looked around to confirm we had found the right cabin. It didn't take long to find the evidence. On the side of an out-building was a wooded sign engraved with Gerhard's family name! I took a photo of Jo and Just Sue to prove that we had been there and left one of our cards in the door, and we headed off in great spirits to retrace our steps back to the road south and our mission in the Alps. We were sorry to have missed seeing them, but knew it was highly improbable they would have been there for our unannounced visit. A day later, however, we got a text message from Gerhard. They had arrived back at the cabin later in the day and we had missed them by only a few hours.

All of this mucking about looking for cabins in the mountains was starting to pay dividends. The three of us—me, Jo and Just Sue—were getting used to the mountain roads and the difficult conditions for riders. Tracks like the one up to the mountain cabin were certainly challenging on a bike, but ahead of us was a different type of experience altogether: the Grossglockner Hochalpenstrasse. This is a legendary motorcycle road, so famous that they've put a toll gate at either end, charging a fee to ride it! The pass has been used for more than 2,000 years and was once among the most important passes in the Alps. The tourist brochure handed out at the toll gate lists pre-Celtic bronze knives, Celtic gold jewellery, a Roman Hercules statue, medieval pack-animal bridles and the chains of galley slaves from the 17th century among the archaeological finds that have been made along its route. By the 17th century, it was second in importance only to the Brenner and the Radstadt Tavern, but these days commercial traffic goes through all-weather tunnels, so the mountain road has been turned over to tourism. The modern Hochalpenstrasse (high alpine road) we were riding had been built between 1930 and 1935 according to plans by the engineer Franz Wallack.

We had ridden over the Grossglockner Hochalpenstrasse a few years before during an earlier trip to Austria. That had been a dark, brooding day, and the pass had been closed by snow the previous evening. There were few other vehicles at the toll gates paying the 18 euros to use the road, and it was so wide and empty that we'd blasted our bike away from the gates at full throttle, enjoying the chance to use all of its substantial acceleration. It was an amazing ride to the top over an excellent surface, with a mix of tight hairpin bends and open sweepers climbing relentlessly to the pass. I remember gathering up a few slower riders easily between the corners and arriving at the mist-shrouded top, the Edelweissspitze, grinning like a loon. Jo took a photo of me standing beneath the Edelweissspitze sign, rugged up against the cold with my beanie pulled down over my ears and the clouds hanging heavy behind.

Then we'd taken a detour out to a huge parking area (much of it undercover) called Franz Josef's Hohe, which had a view of both Grossglockner (3770m) and the Pasterze Glacier. With a strong wind blowing off the ice, it was bitterly cold. Bikes were parked down the roadside, spilling out of the car park and using every available space; it seemed every motorbike in southern Austria had somehow ended up there. Under an awning on one side of the parking area, banks of lockers provided somewhere to stow helmets and heavy riding gear, and riders enjoyed a hot chocolate in the glass-walled café just below. The glacier was right there, right in front of us, filling the valley—huge, misty, brooding and chilling. It was cold enough for us to leave our riding gear on, including our helmets, while we recorded the eerie scene in the swirling mist.

By the time we'd arrived at the southern side of the pass, we felt like our 18 euros had been pretty good value. As we approached the toll gates, a group of German sportsbike riders had slowed, turned before the gates and gunned their bikes back towards the pass, determined to get as many crossings for their money as they could fit into a day. We would have done the same, but we'd already had a long day in the saddle, and it was past time we should have been looking for some accommodation. Even with a single crossing, it had been a grand ride, as spectacular and thrilling as we could have wished for, and we'd passed through the gates feeling pleased with the world.

It is probable that, after that first experience, our memory of Grossglockner was so positive that we were bound to be disappointed the next time round. On our second visit, a clear, hot, mid-summer day, tourists were lined up in all manner of vehicle to get onto the road. We stopped short and looked at the heavy traffic—this would be no merry romp up the mountain this time. Still, we rationalised, better to ride over Grossglockner Hochalpenstrasse than take a lesser pass. Our faith was still intact until we sidled up to the toll gates and discovered the price had gone up to 23 euros. After that, things just got messy.

A kilometre up the mountain we found ourselves baulked by a phalanx of erratic white hatchbacks, and it was the same all the way up the hill; bewildered tourists in little cars, lunatics in sports cars and cruiser-bike riders going so slowly I was sure they would fall over.

I was hot and bothered by the time I found a place in the crowded car park to take the necessary photographs. Jo snapped a picture to match the one from our previous visit. In this one, I have a forced smile and look like I would rather be somewhere else, ideally somewhere with cold beer. We made one final stop so that Jo, ever the scientist, could collect a rock sample from the summit, and then we joined the steady stream of holiday traffic down to the mountain, to intersect with our track near Lienz from a few days before.

For us, the Grossglockner has been both the best and the worst of motorcycle roads. On a perfect day, it was awe-inspiring, but locked into a parade of unpredictable, meandering Fiat Puntos, it was like having teeth drilled. Our advice would be to pick your time carefully. Go in spring, before the holidays, or in autumn when everyone is back at work and the weather is bad enough to keep the fainthearted indoors. Then go early in the day. Spend the first trip over stopping for the view and photographs, and enjoy watching the other bikes as they carve up through the bends. Turn around at the toll gates and ride back to see it all from the other direction. Then make your final run without a stop, just for the sheer bloody fun of it.

For our part, we made a run to Lienz, and found some comfortable accommodation and comforting food. Over dinner, we considered the options. We could loop north again and continue criss-crossing Austria, or head south into Italy and the

Dolomites. We discussed the options for an hour before finally deciding our earnestness was a little silly. If this was our most pressing concern, we didn't have much to complain about. We flipped a coin and settled on Italy.

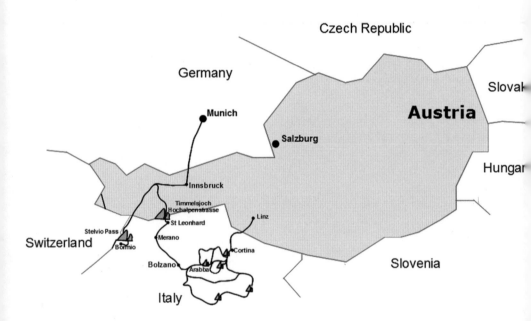

5

THE DOLOMITES AND THE SEARCH FOR ANDREAS HOFER

We dropped into the north of Italy, near the town of Innichen, northeast of the famous holiday destination Cortina. This part of the Alps is known as the Dolomites (Dolomiti in Italian or Dolomiten in German), distributed between the provinces of Belluno, Sud Tyrol and Trentino. The mountains are named after the mineral dolomite, which is the major component in the dolostone that makes up the Alps. The mineral was in turn named after Italian geologist Déodat Gratet de Dolomieu (1750–1801), who first described the rock from these mountains.

We settled ourselves in roughly the centre of the Dolomites, in the town of Arabba, which seemed to be handy to a maze of mountain roads and a number of important passes. John Hermann describes a route around Arabba that would cross 17 passes in a single day; while I'm sure we know some riders who would be keen to try this feat, we didn't give it a second thought. For us, motorcycle travel has never been about how far we could go, how many borders we could cross or how many boxes we could tick. We know we can ride for 16 hours with only fuel stops and sleep by the road if we need to, but that isn't much fun, and it's dangerous. Instead, we settled for a modest meal and a glass of wine in a local café, and made a lazy start the next morning.

Leaving Arabba, the Passo Pordoi began at the edge of town. We had started the day relaxed and chatty and were still settling down to business when I looked up at the end of the main street and the road disappeared into an uphill hairpin. I remember thinking, 'Hell, I'm not ready for this yet', as the corner loomed up far more quickly than I expected. I hauled Just Sue through the switchback, exiting a little early and wide, cursing quietly. I shook myself to relax the sudden tension in my shoulders and then settled to the task of reeling another dozen switchbacks on the way to the top of the Pass. By the time we had a quick photo stop to look back on a now distant village, I had decided that this was going to be a very good day at the office.

The road down from Passo Pordoi led seamlessly to the start of Passo di Sella, which delivered us onto the old Dolomite Road running east to Cortina. This is a popular tourist route and we found ourselves grinding along behind one tour bus after another. Each had a long tail of little cars, which required negotiation, until we were close enough to use the size and acceleration of the bike to slip by the bus. After a short romp, we would come to the back of another tail of cars, following another bus. It was starting to dawn on us that the Dolomites were overrun by tourists in the summer, and that our vision of isolation in the pristine mountains wasn't quite going to match the reality. We hadn't been expecting so much traffic and it did take the gloss off an otherwise wonderful ride.

By the time we climbed over Passo di Gardena, we'd adopted a more relaxed attitude to the traffic. We didn't grind along at the back but nor did we take every opportunity to overtake. We slipped by when it was easy and safe, drifted along behind when it wasn't, and didn't look too hard for opportunities. That night when I prepared a post for our blog, I noted that the Dolomites would be an excellent place for a romantic holiday touring around in an open-topped sports car, and recommended a well-restored MGB or a Mazda MX5 as about the right tone. I then went on to warn against a Porsche or, the worst possible option, a Ferrari. It seemed to me that nothing would be more likely to make you look silly than sitting behind a line of little cars and a bus, in a snarling supercar, unable to pass.

By the end of that first day around Arabba, we had added Passo di Valparola, Passo di Falzarego and Passo Campolongo to our growing list of bagged passes. Despite the traffic on some parts of the circuit, we found other sections relatively deserted and easy riding. In some places, there were even picnic tables in clearings by the road, where the well-prepared could enjoy a relaxed lunch break. At least, that was always the plan. As with most of Europe, the Italians don't often provide toilet facilities at picnic stops, and a brief walk was usually all it took for us to realise that these were often decidedly unhealthy and unpleasant places. We have seen the same filthy sites all across Europe and have never understood why the locals put up with it.

On this first loop, north-east of Arabba, we also made some historical discoveries when we stopped in a parking area near a monument on Passo di Valparola. We hadn't intended to stop, but it was a convenient place to pull off the road, stretch our legs and have a drink. Jo climbed off while I sorted Just Sue, then climbed off myself. She stopped suddenly and stared at a monument next to the parking area.

'What's wrong?' I asked.

'That statue, it moved', she said. 'It's not a statue at all.'

When I looked up I could see what had drawn her attention. What appeared at first to be a statue of an Italian soldier in WWI dress was a live soldier standing guard on the top of a bunker. We had stumbled, almost literally, upon the Museum of the Tre Sassi Fort and a continuation of the World War I history that had dominated our time in the eastern Alps.

It was a reminder that many of the roads we were traversing owed their existence to World War I and the need to resupply the Italian and Austrian fronts. This area has been part of that long arc of battlegrounds, stretching from the Swiss frontier to our west, all the way to the Adriatic. It was a warm, comfortable day, but looking around at the towering limestone mountains, it didn't take too much imagination to see this place covered in snow and ice, beset by a howling wind. It would be hard to find any place worse to fight a war and I could only wonder what the uneducated peasants from the south, who fought in many of the early battles, would have thought of the place. For those simple men, agricultural land was the only true measure of wealth, and by that measure this place was worthless.

As we had discovered in Slovenia, the Italians had come to the Alps with imperialistic intentions. It was an obsession that had proven costly, in human suffering and wasted resources, and contributed little to the developing sense of Italian national identity. The disillusion of wartime failure also contributed to the rise of Mussolini and the Fascists. Although the decisive battles of that campaign had been fought in the east, some of the harshest conditions and most bitter fighting had been in the north, where the climate and the very mountains themselves were much more likely to kill a soldier than the enemy. On just one day, 16 December 1916, avalanches killed 10,000 soldiers on this front. The day became known as White Friday. In his book *The White War*, the historian Mark Thompson describes the conditions on the battlefield as 'a third army, one that would kill them all, given a chance'.[5] And it wasn't only the cold and the altitude that were dangerous; artillery shells detonating on the stony ground of the Alps were 70 per cent more effective than those fired into the soft soils of Flanders, where the ground would absorb much of the blast and fragmentation. Unlike the Western Front, where field hospitals could be maintained close behind the lines with a organised system of casualty evacuation, a wounded man here could suffer gruelling days being carried by porters down to a medical facility.

Suffering horrific conditions and with no apparent end to the fighting, the nationalist fervour that had contributed to Italy's entry into the war was never going to be sufficient motivation to continue the fight. Desertions were commonplace and many units withdrew rather than face defeat. This became such a problem that the Italian commander General Luigi Cadorna ordered the decimation of any unit found to have retreated from the enemy. Decimated—it is such a common word these days. We talk of football teams being decimated in a game, or a population of wildlife having been decimated, but the word has a much more sinister and precise meaning, ancient and military in origin. If a Roman unit was 'decimated', it meant that one man in ten would be selected at random and killed, not for anything that man had done, but as an example to the others. There have only been a handful of cases of decimation in modern times—there is a Russian example from Stalingrad, and undocumented rumours of others, so Cadorna's order stands out as extraordinary. Decimation reflected a failure of leadership and is recognition of the fact that, for Italian soldiers of 1917, there was nothing worth fighting for in the Alps.

Cardona's order notwithstanding, there were many examples of Italian units who fought with great bravery even, in one notable case, to the last man, when their own headquarters decamped, leaving them unsupported. The fate of the Northern Front was not, however, decided by the bravery of the troops, but rather by events in the eastern Alps. The Italian loss at the Battle of Caporetto in 1917 realigned the front far to the south. By the last weeks of the war in 1918, with detailed planning and a new, capable and cautious commander, the Italians finally launched a successful counteroffensive, driving the front north and east. By this time the Austro-Hungarian Empire was exhausted and on the verge of collapse and the loss of many thousands of troops, taken prisoner by the Italians, was enough to bring on the end. The Italians were finally able to march to the mountains in the north and Trieste in the east to claim them for Italy.

The Museum of the Tre Sassi Fort has a collection of equipment and armaments from the period, which are well and thoughtfully presented. In addition, there are extensive walking trails through the mountains that use the old World War I resupply routes, some of which were covered to provide protection from both snow and shell fire. Old World War I defensive works are still intact and protected for the interested tourist, easily accessible and worthwhile to visit. It is all tastefully done, and it seemed to us that the war in the mountains had come to be seen less through the lens of Italian or Austrian nationalism, and more as a common disaster with many victims and no real victors. It is no doubt best remembered this way.

A few days later, the track of our route around Arabba looked like a four-leaf clover, with leaves of various sizes to the north and the south. We did, of course, get all seventeen of John Hermann's passes and a few more for the hell of it. The Dolomites have plenty of them, as well as plenty of spectacular white mountains, including the huge block of limestone called Marmolada, plenty of picturesque mountain villages, and plenty of stunning alpine roads linking them all together.

As we twisted and turned across the Dolomites we started to get a better understanding of the region and its history, and were continually surprised by the natural beauty of these mountains. No matter how jaded a traveller you might be (and Team Elephant can be a little jaded at times), you will find the Dolomites stunning. The mountains soar, the villages cling to hills, the roads defy commonsense and the stunning vista is so commonplace that it hardly warrants a photo stop. Not everyone comes to these mountains for the natural beauty, but I suspect that all who travel here are affected by it. Skiers come to the resorts in winter, but the summer truly brings the Dolomites alive with walkers, cyclists, rock climbers, young romantics, bus-touring retirees and motorcycles by the hundred. You could argue that the area is crowded and a little grubby, and that the facilities are well below the standard seen in other places, all of which would be true, but a little churlish. Whatever the shortcomings of Dolomite plumbing, visitors are swept along by the area's simple magnificence.

The Dolomites were such a fascinating adventure for us that we kept looping back on our route to ensure we covered as much of the area as we could. Despite our wanderings, we moved inexorably west, until we had entered the part of the mountains that lay within the autonomous Italian province of South Tyrol (German and local Ladin: *Südtirol*, Italian: *Sudtirolo*). We had been told this area was known as 'German-speaking Italy', as it had been part of the Austro-Hungarian Empire until 1918. This, however, proved to be simplistic. The first person we spoke to was a woman in her thirties, who claimed her family spoke Ladin dialect at home, German in the village and Italian when it was needed. Her English was also fair because of her work with the winter ski business. She described how her father, who would have been about my age, was banned from speaking anything other than Italian at school in the 1950s, and how efforts to suppress the regional language had been continued until the late 1970s. It was the sort of conversation that always piques our curiosity and in this case led us to stay a while.

We rode on a little but pulled off the road to the pass known as Timmelsjoch on a sulky, wet afternoon and into the small village of St Leonhard, set back in the foothills. At the information office we found a list of the cheap pensions, identified the few that were in our price range and available that time of year, and set out to find the most likely place for a bed. A map from the information office directed us higher up the hill and further into the woods, to a two-storey house of heavy, dark timber, in the alpine post-and-beam style, with a large comfortable room for us.

We walked back to the village and started to take stock of the place. This was Italy, but an Italy where the people spoke German or a dialect we couldn't identify, where the houses and clothing were alpine, a place of mountain cheeses and heavy breads, a place where men in lederhosen and Tyrolean hats were unremarkable. It was different to any other part of the country we had seen, but this was hardly a surprise. Italy is defined by its provinces, each of which has distinct regional differences, including unique dialects in some cases.

The long unification of modern Italy, starting in the middle of the 19th century as the Risorgimento, was not fully complete until well into the 20th century and many feel it remains a work in progress. We had no trouble finding Italians from the northern provinces who strongly believe Garibaldi should never have gone to Sicily to unify Italy in 1860, and that the north and south of the peninsula should be separate countries. The often unspoken subtext is that the south is innately African and a poor fit with the industrialised, European, 'cultured' north. I remember, from my childhood in an impoverished inner Sydney suburb, that the same prejudice had been applied to the New World. The northern Italian immigrants were fine, they were like us, but those from the south were somehow different. Indeed, those who turned up for school without such essentials as shoes were made to parade in a separate group, and called the Garibaldies. Such was the casual racism of my youth.

But in South Tyrol, there was more to the differences than a simple north–south prejudice. Here was a part of the north that was uncomfortable with its connection to the remainder of the north, and remote from the south. Perhaps this is not surprising. Throughout the long history of the peninsula, even the idea of a united Italy had never pressed this far north, and the Romans never incorporated this land into the Empire. By the year 1490, the cluster of principalities considered to occupy the land of Italy ended at Lake Garda, with the Venetian Republic extending to the north-east, and Milan to the west and the Swiss border. In 1815, a meeting of the foreign ministers of European states, brought together in Vienna by Austrian statesman Klemens Wenzel von Metternich, agreed the areas of the member states with no change to this northern border. It remained this way throughout the eventual Risorgimento. There is a monument in Bonzner Platz in Innsbruck, the only important city in the Tyrol, erected in 1877 to mark 500 years of the unification of the Tyrol with Austria. Today, Austria controls only the provinces of Osttirol (East Tyrol) and Tyrol, which are now separated by the Italian province of Sudtirolo.

As I dragged the bags into our B&B in St Leonhard, I noticed a painting of a man in classic Tyrolean kit, which took pride of place in the entry foyer. He seemed to supervise my clumsy baggage handling with steely eyes, looking out from under a broad-brimmed hat, and with his strong chin there was clearly no Hapsburg blood there. I asked our host who the ancestor was. 'Andreas Hofer!' answered the frau, with such force I was left in no doubt she thought I was an ignorant idiot. I smiled and nodded and wrote down the name in my notebook. We found many other images of Hofer in Italian South Tyrol, but also in the Austrian states of Tyrol and East Tyrol. He was always portrayed in traditional Tyrolean dress, sometimes brandishing a sword, but more often it was some version of the print we had seen in St Leonhard, Hofer's fixed gaze directed at the onlooker.

The basic facts on Hofer were easy to find. He was a sometimes-wine merchant, smuggler and innkeeper, who took up arms against Bavarian rule for the cause of the Tyrol. The French had granted the Tyrol to the King of Bavaria as a reward for his support against Austria in the Battle of Austerlitz in 1805. In 1809, the Tyrol rose against the king and Hofer led an army to a famous victory at Bergisel, now in the suburbs of Innsbruck near to the ski ramp established for the 1974 Winter Olympics. Hofer briefly established a Tyrolean government in Innsbruck before a military setback sent him into hiding. As is often the fate of such revolutionaries, he was betrayed by a farmer for 1,500 gilders, and executed by the far more revolutionary French. According to folklore, at his appointment with a firing squad, Hofer refused a blindfold, shook the hand of the corporal in charge, gave him a generous tip and told him to 'shoot straight'. With swagger like that, it's no wonder he remains a charismatic Tyrolean hero.

On the morning of our departure from St Leonhard, we settled for breakfast in what would once have been the family room of the old house. The walls were covered with several dozen mounted deer heads, including several stags with nice points. 'Hell,' I said, 'the bastards shot Bambi.' Jo tried to stifle a laugh, to save embarrassment with the frau in the kitchen, but when I looked over at her I saw the stuffed figure of a small fawn, standing not more than 25cm high at the withers and centrally placed on an ornate dresser. I pointed to it and blurted out, 'They really did shoot Bambi!' We were still laughing when our breakfast was brought in by a bemused landlady.

By the time we finished breakfast, we had decided it would be good to hunt out some more information about our new friend Andreas Hofer. It was this simple decision that dictated our onward journey. We reprogrammed our GPS for the Timmelsjoch, the pass into Austria. Beyond it lay Innsbruck, the 'capital' of the Tyrol, Hofer's resting place and home of the Hofer legend. I looked at the painting again as I dragged our bags back through the foyer. On second inspection, Andreas had the hint of a cheeky smirk.

The Timmelsjoch is another of those legendary passes that make riders put silly stickers on their panniers to brag about having been there. For more than 6,000 years, shepherds used this route over the mountains from the Passeiertal valley in Italian South Tyrol to the Ötztal valley in the Austrian province of Tyrol. The name Thymelsjoch was first documented as far back as 1241, some 50 years before the first historical record of the more famous Brenner Pass. It was only a little south-west of here, in 1991, that the body of the Neolithic man named Ötzi was found protruding from the ice of the Similaun Glacier. Ötzi was named after the Ötztal valley and has been carbon dated to 3,500 BC.

The modern road was started in 1955 but had a long and tortured history stretching back to the 19th century. The need for a quality road had long been recognised and it might well have been constructed in the early years of the 20th century if not for World War I. The Italian takeover of South Tyrol made the Timmelsjoch a national border, complicating the agreement between local governments on either side of the new border. By the middle of the century local politicians realised the importance of a new road and the necessary funds to start construction were procured. At the top of the pass, there is an excellent display that outlines much of this history, as well as a photo collection documenting the construction. As the Timmelsjoch was the first road in the Alps to be constructed using heavy machinery rather than manpower, the display was worth a short visit. Some of the difficult conditions under which the early bulldozers worked were amazing. The road itself lived up to its reputation and provided us with a chilly and thrilling ride into Austria.

A fast, open ride north brought us to the main east–west road near the Austrian town of Haiming. We then turned west, shadowing the motorway for a few kilometres, before turning south again on a minor rural road. By the time we joined the main road heading back to Italy through the Reschenpass, we had used up half of the day. It was an easy climb into a low pass (1,500m); we were not surprised to discover that this had been a well-used footpath since before Roman times, and that the current pass was once part of the Via Claudia Augusta, which opened for business in 50 CE. By the time we reached an overnight stop in the Italian town of Burgeis, we were only about 50km from our start pointing at St Leonhard, despite having ridden more than 200km over two well-known passes. We didn't seem to be making much progress with our zig-zag track. A half-hour's ride to the south of Burgeis, just north of the Italian ski town of Bormio, was the legendary Stelvio Pass with its 60 hairpin turns and we wanted to be rested to get the best out of the experience the following day.

The Stelvio was built by the Austro-Hungarians in the early 19th century. At 2757m, it is one of the highest passes in the Alps, and is frequently closed by snowfalls. We arrived in the crisp of the morning and launched into the 48 hairpins that clamber up from the northern side, with the confidence born of more than a month in the Alps on a motorcycle. But even after so many previous passes, getting the cornering technique just right for so many hairpins in such quick succession was a challenge—an exhilarating, mind-focussing challenge. The road was narrow and badly maintained and reflected its old survey, but we were at the top within an hour, including several stops for photography. There we found a pass still bordered by snow and alive with activity. The road was lined with souvenir and food stalls and dozens of people were already there, including cyclists, bikers, sports car drivers and the ubiquitous bus groups. The bratwurst and beer stands were doing a roaring trade and several substantial restaurants and cafés were well patronised. There was even a bank, open for business, just in case you needed a loan to pay for your bus fare home.

We found a café a little further up from the pass, with a great view back to the north, so parked Just Sue in the snow outside and ordered hot chocolate and strudel. Now, many are under the impression that hot chocolate in the Alps, particularly Swiss hot chocolate, is of especially excellent quality. This, unfortunately, is not the case and the powdered version we drank on the Stelvio was typical of the stuff served up in most establishments. For the best hot chocolate, go to Spain, where it is almost universally good and irresistible when served with fresh hot churros.

Suitably refreshed by whatever chemicals are to be found in artificial hot chocolate, we purchased a Stelvio Pass sticker from a tourist stall, and Jo collected a piece of Stelvio rock from the cutting. Later we would put these in a small presentation box for friends who had been unable to ride the pass due to snow. We knew they were very disappointed when they missed the experience and the gift would only make them feel worse—none of which deterred us for a moment from the joke! With the sticker and rock stowed in the tank bag, we launched Just Sue down the switchbacks on the southern side of the pass, heading for a lunch break near the town of Bormio before turning around and riding back through the pass in the opposite direction. The weather had closed in by the time we were back at the top, but the pass circus was still in full swing, and we were left to wonder how bad the weather would have to get before the customers stayed in the valley. We retraced our steps north through Mals and over the Rechenpass and turned east at the valley road. From there, it was back to plainer, slower, busier roads, drifting east and eventually on to Innsbruck.

Innsbruck is tourist-central for the Tyrol. It is full of people clutching digital cameras and standing on corners looking bewildered with their map upside down. Like all tourist destinations, there was no end of kitsch to celebrate the region and its history. Indeed, the unwary tourist might end up with a full Tyrolean suit, including one of those fantastic broad-brimmed hats. I say unwary because there is always a trap in buying a hat when you don't fully understand its provenance. Hats, you see, above other forms of dress, are traditionally used to designate rank and status—and it just doesn't seem right to turn up at your next party dressed in a hat worn only to funerals and church. None of this, however, bothered us much. We had a mission—we were looking for something of Andreas Hofer.

Our first task was to catch a local tram out to Bergisel, the place where Hofer's Tirolean uprising had it finest hour. Hofer's success at Bergisel was recorded in 1896 in a huge painted panorama, which has recently been restored and moved to a modern, purpose-built museum near the site of the battle. The original location was in a building near the river in the city of Innsbruck itself. It is a vastly overblown and heroic work, from a time when the expression of such nationalist sentiment did not need to be accompanied by any reverence for the facts. Nonetheless, the painting provides a good feel for the chaos and confusion of battles at that time (or any time really), and allowed us to identify many of the Tirolean nationalists who played a part in those events. It also showed us why the Tiroleans had won the day—they clearly had the best hats!

The museum also housed several portraits of Hofer, including the one we had seen reproduced in the house in St Leonhard. We took our time over the display, making notes and taking carefully framed photographs to record our findings, then enjoyed the view over an expensive lunch in the museum restaurant. In the park near the museum is another late 19th century monument of Hofer, also of heroic proportions, but expressing quite different sentiment. The bronze shows a swashbuckling Hofer, very different from the man in the portrait. The piercing gaze was missing and the hat sat at a cocky angle. Then there was the inscription: For God, Kaiser and the Fatherland. I am not sure about Hofer's view on the Almighty, but as a Tyrolean to the core, we can be sure he knew the Kaiser could take care of himself.

Hofer is buried in a church that also contains the tomb of Emperor Maximilian I. Maximilian's tomb is an extravagant monument, surrounded by 28 life-size bronzes of the European kings and queens who were his contemporaries, as well as those of antiquity and legend. The aim was clearly to establish the divine rights of this minor potentate by associating him with current and past legitimate rulers. No expense was spared and the detail in the statues is exquisite and no doubt costly. I was most taken by the statue of King Arthur of the Britons and the small dragons embossed on his armour. It seems little wonder that the legend of this mythical character remains strong, as he has such a strongly defined image in art.

Hofer's grave is in a nearby corner and is a far less grand affair. He was, after all, just a local freedom fighter who was betrayed and shot. The laugh, however, was on Maximilian, because Hofer is actually buried in the church, while Maximilian is not. The emperor's tomb is empty—his entourage was refused entry by the city burghers because his soldiers hadn't paid their bills—and he is buried near Vienna in a much plainer grave. This small fact was missing from the fancy sound and light show and the enthusiastic presentations of the guides for the thousands of tourists who had flocked to see Maximilian's mausoleum. It did, however, bring a smile to a couple of scruffy bikers watching the tour groups from the choir loft above the altar.

Our brief sojourn to Innsbruck in search of Andreas also set the scene for a more personal drama. A couple of days idling around this pleasant Tyrolean city had allowed us to recover after several weeks of constant travel, and to avoid being on the bike during a period of extremely hot weather, a feature of the summer of 2012. We were just packing to head back to the mountains when Jo received word that her mother, who was 97, had had a stroke and was not expected to live.

We laid out our maps and started to make a new plan. The nearest airport with good connections to Sydney was Munich, a few hours ride over the mountains. We booked a ticket to Sydney for Jo, packed the bike and started north. At this point, with the sort of compounded luck that makes our lives interesting, the weather turned and it started to rain. Despite the wet roads, we took the back way over the mountains and trundled north in a steady stream of traffic. An easy, picturesque ride over Scharnitzpass, past lakes Walchansee and Kochelsee, dropped us down onto the rolling farmland south of Penzberg. By then the rain had eased and a steady breeze was drying the road.

'Did you see that barn?' Jo's intercom crackled in my helmet after a long silence.

'What was it?'

'There was a sign painted on a wall facing the road. If my German is correct it said: South Tyrol is not Italian.'

This was more than enough to keep us chatting until the Saturday traffic in Munich brought us back to the more prosaic business of keeping the bike out of harm's way and getting ourselves into a hotel close to the airport. We spent a long and vacant Sunday, interred in a business hotel close to the airport, somewhere in that great swath of industrial parkland that rings the city. In a town where everything closes on Sunday, we were lucky to find a store where we could buy a canvas bag for Jo's few possessions. On the Monday morning we had a late breakfast in a local village before I rode out to the airport. As I watched Jo walk away towards the Munich terminal, I knew she had long hours locked in the back of a plane ahead of her, flying with the worst airline in the developed world, so I wished her good luck and turned back to Just Sue. Later in the week, I wrote in our blog that I was struck by what you can get good at in life, and how it isn't always what you expect.

By the time Jo had arrived in Sydney, her mother Clare Lobban had passed, but she was in time for the funeral arrangements and the wake. Clare had had a fine long life and kept her faculties and good health until the end, so there was much to be thankful for along with the sadness. Jo and her sisters saw their mother sent off in style, while the remnants of Team Elephant returned to the mountains, where life suddenly became difficult.

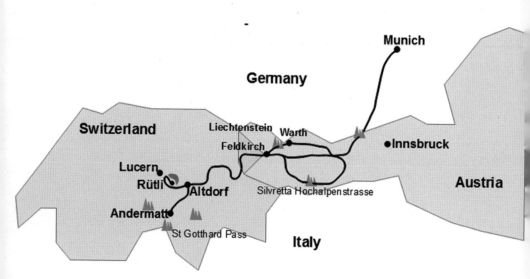

6

WILLIAM TELL AND THE MAKING OF SWITZERLAND

I climbed onto Just Sue, took two deep breaths, and steeled myself for a run across the city on slimy-wet roads. The mountains were to the south and that was the way I needed to go.

An hour-and-a-half later, I was back in Austria and climbing over the Fernpass south of Ehrwald. I dropped down into the Bruck River Valley west of Innsbruck and turned north-west on the back roads. My return to the Austrian Tyrol also brought me back to the wider story of the Tyrol that had, it seems, taken over our journey. Whatever the pragmatism of the new EU, it was clear to an outsider that the Italian ownership of South Tyrol was still contested by some. What was difficult to judge was how much real discontent remained. I recalled working in the US state of Georgia some years before and being corrected by the lady of the house I was visiting when I mentioned the American Civil War; in those parts, she pointed out, it was known as Lincoln's War of Yankee Aggression. If this was a joke at my expense, no one laughed, but I also noted that none of that group would have countenanced secession from the union for a moment. This experience gave me cause to wonder about the mindset of the modern population of the South Tyrol, and whether they were reconciled to their Italian future.

After 800 years of Austrian control, it would be surprising if the people of the Tyrol were not ambivalent at best about the Italian rule. Shortly after the 1918 annexation, a pamphlet pleading the cause of Tyrolean independence was published in the United States. The anonymous author questioned the legitimacy of the 1915 Treaty of London (between the United Kingdom, France and Italy) on which the territorial claim was based, then went on to make the case for the German nature of the region. The pamphlet cites an official census of 1910, which records 215,796 German speakers, 15,410 Ladin speakers and only 5,765 Italian speakers. Apart from the cultural argument, the case for Tyrolean difference was also made in terms of security, human rights and defence. Its most persuasive argument, however, was economic. 'Italy is unable to give us that economic and industrial development for which everybody hopes after the war',[6] the author wrote, and that economic argument remains persuasive.

In 2010, 90 years after the question of the Tyrol made this claim, Austria's growing economy generated a GDP per capita 30 per cent higher than Italy's. It was managing unemployment below five per cent, had one of the most equal income distributions in Europe and was in the top 20 countries in the world for this metric. Italy's economy, in comparison, had been stagnating for more than five years with unemployment above 10 per cent overall, and above 20 per cent for the young. The distribution of income across Italian society remains poor by both European and world standards. Even the unobservant traveller need only fly into Rome's creaking airport (particularly out of a modern Asian port) to see the state of the country's crumbling infrastructure and imagine that things will not get better.

I do not intend to make the case that Austria is some latter-day Utopia—far from it. But overall it seems to be running a more successful economy than Italy. It is hard to imagine that any parent of the South Tyrol, faced with the prospect of raising children in a such a bleak economy, would not hold that the question of the Tyrol had not been answered well.

Heading into the west of Austria and keeping an eye out for armed men in lederhosen, I started looking for a base from which to explore Voralberg, the western-most province. I found a good gasthaus in the town of Feldkirch, close to the Liechtenstein border, where I was the only customer and where the beer and food was good, cheap and plentiful. This allowed me a few long days riding a large figure-eight around the mountains to the north and south of the valley road. To the north, the lesser-known road runs west from the town of Imst, brushing the German border near the village of Warth and finally turning south towards Feldkirch at the village of Au. It provided a spectacular day on a motorcycle, which I didn't want to end despite aching shoulders and a sore backside, but it was also an early reminder that the nature of the journey had changed.

In the mid-afternoon I stopped at a small kiosk in a low pass near Warth for a shot of coffee. The place was shrouded in swirling mist, which allowed only glimpses of the view, down long spectacular valleys in either direction. It made me want to huddle in around the hot coffee and tell Jo how spooky I thought it was, but with only Just Sue to share my thoughts, I settled for a photo with the wide-angle lens and rode on feeling something of the specialness of the moment had been missed.

We have always travelled as a couple and over the years have developed a system of responsibilities to divide up the work and give each other some personal space. We have never written the rules down, and would probably have trouble articulating them if asked, but whatever needs to be done gets done. This teamwork comes into its own when things aren't going well. Both of us have been sick or injured on the road and relied completely on the other just to get by. I remember a dose of amoebic dysentery on one trip that left me so weak I could barely ride the bike and couldn't do anything but sleep when we stopped. Another time Jo injured her back in a fall and we spent two weeks lying about in cheap hotels waiting for it to improve.

Some of the divisions of labour are almost laughable. For example, Jo always insists that I do the shopping in countries where we are completely lost for language. Her argument is that the women who invariably serve at the counter find my smiling charades charming and respond with good humour and service, while they are often not well disposed to the same performance from another woman. There may be some truth in this and there is no doubt the way we interact with people we meet when travelling together is different to the way we interact when travelling alone. As a couple, we are self-contained, and people don't feel the need to offer much by way of assistance. As a single, you are seen as incomplete and vulnerable, and people are much more willing to assist. Several adventure riders we know insist on travelling alone because they feel they are better able to link into the local community that way.

There are probably advantages and disadvantages to both options, and that day I was certainly missing Jo, but this was not enough for me to want to link up with any of the other groups I met along the way. We have always preferred to find our own way and never liked riding in a group; we just find it easy not to have to worry about anyone else. Our quip—'If I wanted to ride in a group, I'd catch a bus'—is probably a bit harsh, but our motorcycle friends take it in good humour and mostly leave us to it.

I certainly didn't agonise about this over an excellent dinner and way too much beer at the Feldkirch gasthaus, or as I busied myself with route planning for the following day. The southern loop ran over the famous Silvretta Hochalpenstrasse. This is another of those pay-to-ride roads that have the advantage of being well maintained, but the disadvantage of being very popular with tourists. The information centre claimed 400,000 visitors each year and I am sure most of them were there on the chilly, overcast day when I gunned Just Sue up the mountain. The Silvretta had been constructed as part of the development of a series of dams and hydroelectric plants in the mountains. The first paved road was built in the 1920s to replace an old unpaved cart path and provide access for the trucks needed to build Vermunt Dam. The hydro project and its roads were developed over the next 40 years, but it was not until 1961 that a two-lane road on the current route was opened to the public.

The Hochalpenstrasse itself was a grand ride and well worth the 14 euro fee. The scenery along the road called for many photo stops and the hydro-electric project provided some worthwhile touristic interest on its own. Unfortunately, the journey either side of the mountain road was long and tedious, and the traffic was heavy. By the time I was back in Feldkirch I felt a little let down by the experience. But then again, perhaps it was no worse than many other transit legs we have made over the years, and maybe I was just missing some intercom chat to pass the time. Just Sue was not a great conversationalist.

There was no more of Austria to ride, nowhere to go but Switzerland, and no way to get there except through Liechtenstein—not that I had a problem with Liechtenstein, I just couldn't figure out what its purpose was in modern Europe. It does, however, give a glimpse into an earlier Europe, before the rise of the nation states and strong central governments, as it's the last of a great web of tiny principalities that once made up medieval Europe and the Holy Roman Empire. Europe was surprisingly slow to develop strong national governments. By the 12th century, when Hugo von Liechtenstein inherited an alpine land that would eventually become the principality, China had maintained a central government for more than 1,000 years and the Ottomans for more than 500. Even then, the land was passed between families for another 300 years, until a later Liechtenstein purchased the current principality to gain a position on the German Imperial Diet of Princes.

Francis Fukuyama has written extensively on the origins of political order. He takes the view that the slow development of central government in Europe was caused by the emergence of a strong feudal system, which balanced and limited the rule of kings and led to the development of the rule of law, contributing, eventually, to the development of participatory democracy. Professor Fukuyama's argument is much more complicated and has a great many other factors at play, but he certainly makes the argument that this interminable period as a political backwater was the basis for the freedom we enjoy today: 'For precocious state building in the absence of the rule of law and accountability simply means that states can tyrannize their populations more effectively'.[7]

Perhaps the importance of Liechtenstein, therefore, is that it serves as a reminder of the long gestation of western political order, and of the rules of law and accountability that underpin it. Maybe these things we take for granted deserve a few square kilometres of the Alps as a monument, but whatever altruistic thoughts may have come to me on the ride, they weren't enough to make me stop! I cruised through, well below the posted speed limit, stopping only to buy a Swiss motorway sticker and on the lookout for the notoriously fine-happy local constabulary, crossing into Switzerland without feeling I had missed anything important.

Switzerland is the country most associated with the Alps and has its own alpine foundational myths. So persuasive are the legends surrounding the formation of Switzerland that it was easy to structure my visit around them. With this simple idea as a guide, the first stop had to be the town of Altdorf, custodian of the William Tell legend and all that goes with it. Unsurprisingly, both Altdorf itself, and a larger-than-life statue of Tell in the central square, were easy to find. It was a harder search to find somewhere to park. After 20 minutes circling the centre of town, I pulled Just Sue off onto the edge of a small square, which featured a pretty fountain. On the wall next to my illegal parking place, a poster advertised the annual staging of German playwright Friedrich Schiller's play, *William Tell.* The play, written in 1804, is staged in Altdorf and is the main source for the Tell legend. The production has a cast of hundreds, including many volunteers, and is a great favourite with both Swiss and foreign tourists. Schiller's play was derived from earlier works on the legend and became the model for Rossini's 1829 opera, which gave us the insidious 'William Tell Overture', subsequently appropriated by another masked freedom fighter, who rode a horse named Silver.

The legend tells of how the Austrian tyrant Gessler had a hat placed in the town square of Altdorf, with the order that all were to pay respects as they passed, just as if the hat were Gessler himself. A rugged mountain marksman named William Tell went to Altdorf, refused to genuflect to the hat, and was arrested. Gessler had heard of Tell's reputation as a marksman and offered the infamous bargain that he would be freed if he could shoot an apple from the head of his son. Tell famously made the shot, but incurred the further wrath of Gessler when he made it known that a second crossbow bolt had been made ready to kill Gessler if his son had been harmed. Gessler was incensed and had Tell arrested and bound, but this was only a necessary prerequisite for a daring escape. The steely William went on to lead a peasant uprising against the dastardly Austrians.

This is all good fodder for legends, but it is almost certain that it didn't happen, and that neither Tell nor Gessler even existed. The Tell legend is a reworking of a traditional legend found in several cultures, all of which have a master marksman at their centre who is offered a terrible bargain by a tyrant and makes an impossible shot to save the day. The Danish legend Palnatoki even has the small detail of the second arrow, in that case destined for King Harald, held in reserve in case the first shot missed its mark. Notwithstanding its uncertain basis in fact, the legend of William Tell is the very embodiment of the Swiss character. It is hard to think of any other nation that has so completely embraced its foundational myth.

By the time I had parked and walked back to look at the monument, I was well and truly in the Tell mood. I went past a number of souvenir shops in the surrounding streets, selling all manner of Tell memorabilia, including colourfully illustrated certificates with the legend in archaic print (and several languages) nicely framed in local timber. There were William Tell pocket knives, LED torches, Alpine snow domes and the full range of junk, available everywhere in the world, differentiated only by the Tell name printed on the plastic. The discerning tourist could buy a genuine replica crossbow, just like the one Tell might have used, or a replica pike, like the ones soldiers of the period might have carried. Those wanting to get right in the mood could purchase a range of period costumes. I wondered how many of these things were sold and what the purchasers did with them—were there really houses all over the world with genuine replica William Tell crossbows on the walls, and owners who dressed up like medieval peasants?

The statue by Richard Kissling has been a feature of Altdorf since 1895 and sits in Rathausplatz, the main square, where the arrow shooting incident is supposed to have taken place. The Tell it presents to the world is huge and muscled and has a fatherly hand on the shoulder of his son Walter. The son looks up at his father with sublime reverence, while Tell directs his icy stare at the onlooker, no doubt steeling himself for the fight ahead. I didn't see an apple anywhere. I walked around the statue and looked at it from every angle, but it presented the same steadfast earnestness from every side. There is never much room for subtlety in the legend business.

When Victor Hugo visited the area in 1839 he was thoroughly impressed with the ideas of freedom and equality embodied in the legend. He wrote to his wife:

'I dreamed that I saw the bailiff Gessler stretched out and bleeding in the sunken road, on these primeval boulders slid down from the Rigi, and I heard his dog barking through the trees at the gigantic figure of Tell standing at his full height in the copse.'[8]

Clearly, in the Alps, the notion of the resilient and resourceful individual at the heart of the legend resonates. This has always been a tough land, and before the mid-19th century and the arrival of a harvest of succulent tourists, eking out a living was a precarious business. Mountain soils were poor, the seasons were short and productivity was low without artificial fertiliser. Travellers in the 1860s commented on the poor state of the locals' health and speculated on signs of inbreeding in the isolated mountain valleys. No doubt there was some innate prejudice in these observations from the upper-class English who could afford to travel in those days. The industrial underclass of England was, after all, hardly in ruddy good health at this time, but maybe the writers had more contact with the Swiss poor while travelling than they did with their own at home. An 1864 account of the wealthy traveller of the day is enlightening:

'The family travelled in style, as families of their social standing often did in those times. They drove in an immense barouche, which they chartered on the other side of the Alps, with a courier who smoothed down all the rubs for Mr Crane, and with a lady's maid who kept the long skirts of his daughters duly dusted. They had quantities of veils, air-cushions, and white umbrellas ..."[9]

Kissling's Tell certainly didn't look undernourished to me, so I left him to stare down the beady, digital eyes of a constant flow of tourists, and headed for the William Tell Museum, a few kilometres to the south-west. With six centuries to build on the legend, the museum contains more than enough artwork to illuminate the smallest details of the story. Any lingering doubts about the centrality of Tell to the Swiss was long gone by the time I found Just Sue moping in the car park and went looking for some other parts of the Swiss identity. To find the beginnings of Swiss nationalism, I headed west towards that part of Lake Lucern know as the Urnersee and an isolated meadow on the southern bank.

If Tell is the embodiment of the Swiss character then the Swiss system of government is its practical incarnation. This system contains the ideals of a highly participatory democracy featuring a Federation of Cantons (a canton being a state, or political zone) with limited powers and a fiercely armed independence. It is no surprise that the isolated valleys of the Alps led to the development of strong regional governments if for no other reason than to provide a level of mutual protection from competing communities in surrounding valleys. It may well have remained that way until the cantons were picked off, one by one, by the expanding Hapsburg Empire. What changed things was the opening of the St Gotthard Pass in the early 13th century; I think it's not unreasonable to say that the Gotthard was the making of modern Switzerland, not to mention its first city, Lucern.

Once the pass was open, taxes could be levied on travellers and goods, and a lively trade opened up in the transportation of people and goods, around the lake from Lucern to the village of Flüelen on the south-eastern arm, closest to the pass. It was a good business and the cantons around the lake prospered. As the Gotthard became the main route for traders between Italy and Germany, the prospects for tax revenue increased, and the Hapsburgs started to take an interest in some easy rents. Faced with the Hapsburg threat, the cantonal leaders met on 1 August 1291 (although the exact date is contested) on a meadow at Rütli on the southern bank of the bend in the lake, and signed a pact of mutual assurance and cooperation. Going to Rütli Meadow, therefore, seemed like the next logical step in my exploration of Switzerland.

The idea was good, but getting to Rütli wasn't as easy as it seemed. The meadow is located on a long arm of the south bank, not far from Altdorf. To get there I needed to ride west, well past it on the motorway through a 20km tunnel, then exit and ride back towards the east on the local roads. The sealed road eventually ended in a car park and from there it was a walk in the drizzling rain. I don't know what I expected to find—perhaps some rural version of Rathausplatz—but Rütli Meadow was, in the end, just a meadow. It had a big Swiss flag on an impressive pole, some nicely manicured grass, lots of walking trails and a jetty for the tourist boats. This was just fine by me. Cultural sites don't need to be turned into theme parks, and many would make the pilgrimage to a dune in the desert if it had the significance of Rütli Meadow. The weather and mid-week timing worked in my favour for a change, as I had the place to myself. Normally this would be an invitation to find a comfortable spot in which to partake in a little background reading and contemplation, but the weather soon turned decidedly unpleasant. I walked around briskly, noting that it would have been a better idea to come by boat, then headed back to see if anyone had decided to take off with Just Sue.

Four cantons (Uri, Schwyz, Nidwalden and Obwalden) signed the original pact, and in doing so formed the basis of modern Switzerland. If the retelling in Schiller's 19th century play is to be believed, the representatives of three of the original cantons took a sacred oath at Rütli, where they vowed they wanted to be free, like their fathers, and would rather die than live in slavery. They are stirring words, very much in keeping with the emerging sensitivity of Schiller's time, but I suspect the original signatories were bound together more by the pragmatic necessity of presenting a united front to the Hapsburgs. As Francis Fukuyama has pointed out, peoples throughout history have consistently traded off some of their freedoms for security and this was certainly the case at Rütli.

The confederacy declared itself independent and neutral and quickly expanded to eight cantons including the major cities of Zurich and Bern. It then fought a series of wars to establish its legitimacy and ensure its independence, culminating in the defeat of Maximilian I (that's right, the one not buried at Innsbruck) at Dornach in 1499. By the 16th century it was a nascent democracy, while the remainder of Europe was under the grind of various types of despotism. With the exception of a short stint as Napoleonic Frenchmen, the Swiss have managed to maintain their independence and some form of neutrality ever since. It is no wonder that the foundational myths of the Swiss carry such importance and that the Swiss themselves set such store by them. Rütli Meadow is central to Swiss identity and it was here in 1940, when things in Europe were looking grim, that the Swiss Commander-in-Chief, General Henri Guisan, gathered his entire officer corps. His purpose was to take a solemn oath that reaffirmed these Swiss ideals and would stiffen the officers' resolve in the face of a likely German invasion.

South from these places that lie at the cultural heart of Switzerland, the old road over the St Gotthard Pass has long been replaced by a motorway tunnel of heroic proportions for commercial traffic. Travelling at a more leisurely pace, I turned off the main road to take the ladder of switchbacks up onto the plateau. Unfortunately, a good percentage of the traffic also turned onto the old pass road leaving only the large trucks on the tunnel road. The traffic included a large number of ungainly campers and was quickly reduced to a stop/start crawl. The grinding pace was so slow it was difficult to ride the bike. Moving up a steep slope at a crawl in a car might not be challenging, but it poses a number of problems for a big bike. You simply can't ride that slowly without slipping the clutch and, as I've sometimes tried to explain to officers of the law, bikes fall over if you go too slow. After nearly an hour of this and having climbed only a few kilometres Just Sue was hot, the clutch was stinking and I was worn out. To make matters worse, the weather had changed and the light rain had become a deluge.

The conga line of campers in front of me eventually crested the last pinch and I returned to normal road speed across the plateau. The town of Andermatt was not far ahead sitting astride the old access to the St Gotthard Pass. We had been to Andermatt before. On that occasion, we were chased into town by thundering rain and were happy to find a dry hotel and hot meal. I had found the place a little too touristy and twee for my liking and didn't intend to stay on this second visit. But I was again chased into town by thundering rain and after an exhausting hour lost in the traffic I decided to give the place a second look. With my expectations for the day suitably lowered, I found the tourist office and settled for a comfortable pension just outside of Andermatt and certain to give me some shelter from the worsening storm.

Andermatt is a tourist town and has been serving the travelling public since the Middle Ages, when it controlled access to the St Gotthard Pass. It has all of the usual tourist town stuff including cute narrow streets with slippery cobbles, horse carriage rides around town, plenty of hotels and lots of restaurants serving uninspiring meals at tourist prices. It is also ideally located for bikers intent on riding some of the best roads in Switzerland that radiate out from Andermatt in all directions. Bikers are an important part of the tourist trade and there are a number of *motorad* hotels pitched at biker business. Most of these are indistinguishable from other hotels except for an old bike that is usually mounted on a plinth outside. We have used them from time to time but have generally found them to be aimed at the European weekend riders who are after a comfortable mid-level hotel. Those looking for a budget option generally bypass the *motorad* hotels and head for the pensions.

By the time I had done the grand tour of the little town I was feeling pleased to be there and glad that I was warm and dry. I had even secured Just Sue in a dry garage. The weather had cleared a little so I found a place with a view of the famous Oberalp, the road out to the east—another legendary motorcycle road—and settled with a book and a beer to enjoy the last of the day. Every few minutes a motorcycle would drop down through the last few corners towards the town. I would hear them kick back through a couple of gears then look up to see the bike scything into the last hairpin which ran into a tunnel. I couldn't help but grin as I watched each one disappear into the blackness then reappear, still cranked over with the throttle open, in the main street right in front of me. There were, I thought, not too many better places for an old biker to be.

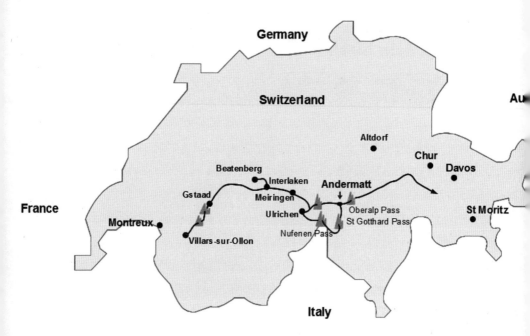

7

THE ENGLISH AND THE RAILWAYS

Whatever Andermatt's failings as the type of cosy backwater preferred by Team Elephant, it was certainly well located for some excellent motorcycle touring. To the east, the Oberalp Pass was touted as the best 'sweeper' road in the world. In the south, the old road over the St Gottard Pass was looking for custom, and to the west, Furka Pass and the Rhône Glacier were waiting for attention. Then there were a dozen minor roads winding up the valleys to more remote villages. As a result, Andermatt was full of bikers and many motorad hotels were doing a brisk trade justifying their tariff by providing lock-up garages for their customers' bikes. Bikers are always happy to stay at a place that offers secure parking and doesn't care if you wear your boots in the lobby on a wet day.

Secure parking may seem like a small thing to the car-driving tourist, but to riders it is a very real benefit. Bikes are easily stolen, even when fitted with alarms and heavy chains. In addition, most riders like to leave some equipment on-board to save lugging it up to a hotel room, which can leave the gear vulnerable to pilfering if not well secured. We are always very careful about where we park, always cover the bike when we are away from it and chain on anything that can be otherwise removed if we are not there to watch it. In North Africa and the Far East, we often found more interesting solutions. Although big bikes were uncommon, innkeepers recognised our dilemma and often agreed to allow us to park in the foyer of the hotel. It is sometimes said that if you can't ride your fully laden machine up four steps then you shouldn't start in the adventure riding game. In other areas 'street wardens' eke out a living earning tips through guarding cars and bikes. We have always made a habit of tipping these folk generously with a good up-front payment to ensure we got conscientious service! Unfortunately, in Switzerland there was never a street warden around when you needed one.

For the next few days the weather ranged from wintry to hot every few hours. Highly changeable weather is common in the mountains and it's best not to worry too much about it. Like the roads, the weather is whatever it is and there is little to be done about it. If we spent our time trying to avoid adverse conditions, no progress would be made. Besides, sometimes a little foul weather can be the making of a journey and this is how it was with the Oberalp Pass.

We had ridden the road previously. The first ride was late in the twilight at the end of a long day and we were full of the expectation of riding one of the great motorcycle roads.

The road was drying, traction was good and the ride, through kilometres of sweeping corners, was great fun even in our saddle-sore condition. Once we could pick a 'dry line' through the corners, Just Sue got her confidence up and started to achieve some impressive lean angles for a big, fully laden bike. The second crack at the Oberalp was a different ride altogether. For the second crossing, it was a cold early morning of 5°C when Just Sue rolled out of Andermatt. Overnight rain had slowed to a wet mist, limiting visibility and giving the place a forlorn feeling. Rather than the late afternoon rush that had driven the first crossing, this ride started with a tentative drive through the edge of town. The early morning traffic was light and most of the Andermatt bikers were still tucked up in their warm beds. Despite the chill and my cold morning stiff joints, it was the ideal time to enjoy the mountains.

Just Sue climbed through the tunnel I had watched the previous evening and on up through the valley with that combination of grace and brutality that makes a tightly ridden big motorcycle a thing of wonder. She fairly romped along, snarling at the little white delivery vans as we flashed past and bellowing echoes off the cutting walls until we flew out along a few kilometres of straight road up to the pass with ears pinned back. By the time I stopped for a shot of coffee at the pass kiosk, thoughts of the cold had vanished, I had a grin from ear to ear and Just Sue was back to her willing self.

Unfortunately, our early morning departure was the best of the day and the remainder of the journey east was much less entertaining. Swiss roads have more than their share of road works and much of the Andermatt–Chur road, which crosses the Oberalp was a construction site, with frequent traffic control stops. The commercial traffic increased steadily as the mist cleared and the tourists finally roused themselves and added motorhomes to the convoy. After the mid-morning coffee break, the elation had evaporated and I was searching in vain for an alternate route.

The Oberalp had been much lauded on the bikers' forums and it was certainly not to be missed. We rode it several more times before the summer was through. But in our view, it is not the 'best sweeper road in the world' it was claimed to be. For us, that award had been won years before by an unnamed road in the Anti-Atlas Mountains of Morocco, which managed to combine wonderful engineering, a good surface, almost no traffic, fantastic scenery, good food along the way, no constabulary and clear winter weather perfect for a motorcycle. Such is the pathetic lot of the adventure rider that we eulogise a long-lost mountain road!

The exploration of the Swiss roads from Andermatt was broken by a long loop through northern Italy. The story of that part of the journey has been gathered up in later chapters on Italy. Our Latin wanderings did, however, eventually bring Team Elephant back to Andermatt and then on to the west of Switzerland. There are so many great bike roads in this part of the country, route planning became difficult as I tried to cover as many roads as I could before the good weather was gone. In addition to the St Gottard and Furka, the Grimselpass, Nufenenpass, Sustenpass and a half dozen lesser roads were within an easy day's round trip. I decided to move the administrative base from Andermatt to the village of Ulrichen a few kilometres to the west where the accommodation might be a little cheaper and the busy work of bagging passes continued.

Along the main valley road past Andermatt I shadowed the route of the famous Glacier Express and often stopped to watch it grind its way along. This railway (reported to be the slowest express train in the world) runs from St Moritz to the south-east of Andermatt to Zermatt, which is in a high valley near the Italian frontier to the south-west. The Glacier Express has operated since about 1930 and shorter sections of the line were working before that. It takes over seven hours to make the journey and uses a cog system for several ascents and descents. It is a favourite with tourists. The express runs through a long tunnel under Furka Pass (one of 91 on the journey) so train travellers never get to see the pass or its glaciers. This, however, seems like a small price for one of the world's most remarkable train journeys.

Trains are everywhere in Switzerland. In such a small country with so many mountains it has more than 5000km of working rail line. It doesn't take long to realise that the railways had been central to the development of the Swiss tourist industry and to Switzerland generally. While this may seem an obvious point, what is more interesting is the role the English played developing the railways and opening Switzerland as a mass tourist destination. It was the industrialised and wealthy English who first had the means to travel and to make tourism a business. The railways then provided the means to democratise travel and started an appetite for alpine tourism that continues today.

It is not that there was no tourism before the railways but it was the preserve of a few hardy adventurers and a class of wealthy rent-takers who didn't have to work for a living. Before the railways, even the wealthy and expanding working middle class did not have the time to travel anywhere exotic in the holidays they could afford to take. It was the development of a European rail network that put the Alps within reach of those with only a few weeks vacation available for travel. Jim Ring has documented the influence of the English in the Alps and he notes succinctly that 'the essential quality of the railway was that for the first time it placed Continental travel within reach of those obliged to work for their living.'[10]

From the mid-19th century, the democratisation of tourism brought about by the railways marked the end of a gradual but relentless shift in the way the mountains came to be imagined. We don't know what the Iceman Ötzi and his contemporaries thought about the Alps, but 2,500 years later in the Middle Ages we know they were seen as the abode of the devil and a place where dragons still lurked. As late as the 18th century, a Swiss professor of physics and mathematics named Johann Jacob Scheuchzer catalogued all of the known species of dragon in the Swiss Alps. As Scheuchzer was a respected scientist and a confidant of Isaac Newton, we can only assume that most people believed in the fearfulness of the mountains. Then, they were certainly not a place near to God nor a place you would go for quiet contemplation. Mountain landscape was also foreign to the medieval eye, which found it harsh, unordered and hostile. In an agrarian society, it is no surprise that verdant flatlands were seen as more beautiful and pleasing to both God and man.

Further to the west we would find evidence of the 18th century romantic notion of the Alps in the popular imagination. But sitting on Just Sue and waving to the tourists on the Glacier Express it was enough to realise that mass transport was needed for mass tourism and here in the Alps that development took on heroic proportions. The Swiss federal government had gained

1 Navigation is a constant task on the road.

2 Jo on the Isle of Man with Australian TT champion Cameron Donald.

3 Bikes line up for the fast ferry from Liverpool to the Isle of Man.

4 TT Week is all about bikes! This is a small gathering at the Creg-Ny-Baa Hotel on the Mountain Course.

5 On the Isle of Man, spectators can get very close to the action.

6 Mike and Jo at Loch Leven, Scotland in a rare break in the rain.

1 Just Sue parked outside the Pilsen Railway Station while Jo looks for the accommodation bureau.

2 Jo beside an elegant bronze of two women sewing the Italian flag on the edge of Trieste harbour.

3 The Soča River Valley from above Kobarid.

1. Mike finds a little shade near a bronze of famous writer and Trieste native Italo Svevo. Svevo was a friend of James Joyce who spent time in Trieste.
2. Ljubljana City Centre is an attractive comfortable place for visitors.
3. Reminders of WWI are spread throughout the mountains. These graves are of Russian prisoners who died constructing the mountain roads.
4. The Russian Orthodox Memorial Chapel on the Vrsic Pass Road was built by Russian prisoners during WWI.
5. Jo explores WWI fortifications near the town of Kobarid.

1 Mike was rugged up against the cold at the Edelweissspritze sign.

2 Mike had never been thanked for riding a motorcycle until he went to Austria!

3 Stopped for the view on the Grossglockner.

4 From the Passo Pordoi looking back towards the town of Arabba over another alpine road that could have been built especially for motorcycles.

5 Jo and Just Sue in the Austrian village of Weissbach near the German border.

6 The Pasterze Glacier. The Grossglockner can be a cold but spectacular ride.

1 Grossglockner Hochalpenstrasse as it approaches the pass.

2 The Grossglockner Hochalpenstrasse is pay-to-ride. €23 buys one of the great motorcycle experiences.

3 The bike parking area near the Pasterze Glacier.

4 Mike and Just Sue at the end of the search for the "cabin in the mountains".

1 The guard at the Museum of the Tre Sassi Fort is dressed in period costume.

2 Jo keeps her warm jacket on to enjoy strudel and hot chocolate in the Stelvio Pass.

3 Typical spectacular Dolomites scenery.

4 Stopped for the view on the Grossglockner.

5 The village of St Leonhard.

6 The road into the Stelvio Pass. One of the great Alpine roads with 48 hairpin bends on the northern side and a further 22 on the southern approach.

1 Maintenance is a constant task on a long motorcycle journey

2 The (empty) tomb of Maximilian I at Innsbruck. The grave of Hofer is just to the right near the tour group.

3 The café at the top of the Stelvio Pass on a clear day.

4 Weather in the Alps is often inclement. Jo puts on her "rubber pants" while we shelter under a service station awning.

1

6

2

5 Idyllic alpine valleys and neat villages are common in the Dolomites. Although this is Italy, the feel is alpine and German.

6 Tourist stalls in the Stelvio Pass. The shirts and nics were popular with those who made the top by bicycle. We settled for a sticker.

3

4

5

1 Andermatt is a tourist town with all the tourist extras including extra high prices.

2 Innsbruck from Bergisel Hill.

3 The hotel in the Furka Pass is now abandoned and the place looks forlorn and deserted.

4 The road towards Feldkirch in western Austria runs through this low pass near the town of Warth.

5. The Rhône Glacier near the Furka Pass west of Andermatt.

1

2

3

5

1 The Silvretta Hochalpenstrasse south east of Feldkirch was €14 to ride but worth the money.

2 A bratwurst stand in the Stelvio Pass.

3 Bikes stop for coffee near Warth in western Austria.

4 West of the Furka Pass near Andermatt, Switzerland.

5 Feldkirch in late spring.

4

1 Conan Doyle Place in the Swiss town of Meiringen is a clue to a little known association between the Scottish writer, tuberculosis and Switzerland.

2 A statue of fictional detective Sherlock Holmes in the Swiss town of Meiringen was erected by the "Norwegian Explorers of Minnesota" and contains clues to 66 Holmes mysteries.

3 The road south from the Nufenen Pass is one of the alpine roads that attracts bike riders from all over the world.

4 View of the Gries Glacier from the Nufenen Pass.

5 St Gotthard Pass has a number of interesting monuments including this one to Russian General Alexander Suvorov.

6 A local produce stall in the St Gotthard Pass was a great place to stock up on cheese and sausage for the week ahead.

1

2

1 Chillon Castle was a minor
attraction except that it gave us
some fine insights into changing
perceptions of the Alps.
2 From my cheap room in
Beatenberg above Interlaken I
had a clear view of the Eiger, the
Mönch and the Jungfrau.

6

3 Jo in Chillon Castle near Montreux.
4 A monument to a Swiss aviator who died
flying over the Alps looks strangely ornate
in St Gotthard Pass.
5 The Silvretta Hochalpenstrasse a little east
of the hydro electric dam that is the reason
for construction of the road.
6 The view from the dungeon in Chillon Castle.

5 3

4

1 The Little St Bernard Pass was less commercialised than the Great version but had this wonderful statue of Bernard warning us back to Italy where the coffee is better.

2 The view through the Great St Bernard Pass.

3 The Maloja Pass was such a hoot that I turned Just Sue around at the bottom and rode up and down again, just because I could.

4 Chiavenna, northern Italy.

5 An encounter with deer hunters in the Albula Pass in Switzerland.

1 Mike by a rented villa in the village of St Didier near the city of Carpentras.

2 There are cyclists everywhere in the Alps. These Saturday morning trainers were in the Gorges du Tarn.

3 As well as great motorcycle roads, the gorges of the Central Massif were a place of great natural beauty.

4 Mike climbed on a wall just below the summit of Mt Ventoux to get a better photo over the scree slope.

5 Alpine roads can be deadly and bike crashes are common.

1 Estaing on the Lot River, French
  Central Massif.
2 The landscape changed markedly
  as we rode south towards the Alpes
  Maritime.
3 a & b. The northern approach to
  Mont Ventoux.
4 Lunch overlooking the Rhone north
  of Pont-Saint-Esprit.

1

1 Mike, Jo and Just Sue on Col d'Izoard.

2 The alpine regions of France started to change as we moved south. This low pass in the Alpes Maritime is typical.

2

3 Many of the older tunnels in the Alps date 100 years and are narrow and dark. This one, south of Briançon, is relatively comfortable.

4 Jo and our daughter Sarah at lunch in Nice

5 Most countries have signs like this. Bikers think they are put up to advise that a good motorcycle road is just up ahead!

6 The village of St Chely-du Tarn.

6

3

5

4

Prudence!

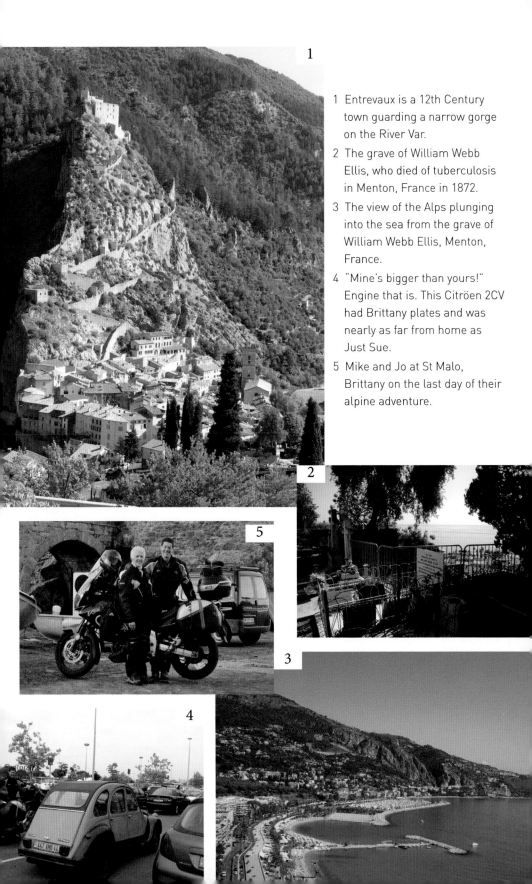

1 Entrevaux is a 12th Century town guarding a narrow gorge on the River Var.

2 The grave of William Webb Ellis, who died of tuberculosis in Menton, France in 1872.

3 The view of the Alps plunging into the sea from the grave of William Webb Ellis, Menton, France.

4 "Mine's bigger than yours!" Engine that is. This Citröen 2CV had Brittany plates and was nearly as far from home as Just Sue.

5 Mike and Jo at St Malo, Brittany on the last day of their alpine adventure.

the power to organise the building and running of railways under the 1848 constitution and contracted two English engineers, Robert Stephenson and Henry Swinburne, to develop a plan for a national rail network. This was expensive help indeed as Stephenson was the son of George Stephenson, the famed railway engineer, and was responsible for a good part of the innovation credited to his father. An extensive plan was drawn up using the valleys and avoiding the high mountains.

Notwithstanding this good start, in 1852, control of the rail system was passed to the cantons who, not unexpectedly and despite federal supervision, made notably parochial decisions. The result was duplication of lines and poor profitability for many companies. Cantons didn't always make the best decisions for the routes of new lines. For example, they insisted on servicing towns in the hills where lines were expensive to build and unprofitable. The performance of the railways emerged in public political debate after problems coordinating the movement of troops for the Franco-Prussian War of 1870–71. By the end of that century the useless work and inefficiency born of local interest was clear to all and a two-thirds majority at referendum handed control of the railways back to the federal government.

This may sound like a chaotic development plan but by the time the railways were nationalised, most of the Stephenson/ Swinburne Plan had been implemented, mostly through the initiate of private enterprise companies. And, the fact that standard gauge (4ft 8½in) was mandated from 1852 compares well with contemporary railway development in Australia where three adjoining states managed to build extensive networks in three different railway gauges. In Switzerland, exceptions to the standard-gauge rule allowed a number of regional mountain railways to be built in a more appropriate track width without compromising the network. The Glacier Express ran on one of these narrow gauge lines with a track of one metre.

The new base in Ulrichen was well located at the intersection of the Nufenen Pass Road but was not much more budget friendly than Andermatt. After a long search I found a tiny pension on the edge of town and pulled up outside. The landlady opened an upstairs window and asked what I wanted in German. I indicated that I needed a room. She gave me a price that seemed very reasonable indeed for Switzerland. I agreed, parked Just Sue, unpacked and made my way inside. It was only then that I realised the cheap price was for a particularly nasty room and no breakfast. This would never have happened if Jo had been with us. I thought about repacking and moving to another place for a moment but then decided on a biker's solution. I threw my gear on the bed and headed off to spend the savings on a better than average meal and some wine that came in a bottle for a change. This seemed like the ideal balance as I wandered home from the pub under a blazing late night sky but I was a little less enthusiastic in the cold light of day with a mild headache and no chance of breakfast.

There was nothing else for it but to hurry to the café I knew would be waiting in Nufenen Pass, a short ride back to the west. At 2478m, Nufenen is one of the highest passes in the Alps and is well regarded by European bikers. I got Just Sue cranked up as soon as I could get my gear in the pannier. By then I had been riding in the mountains long enough to realise that Nufenen road had been surveyed recently and, as a result, had a sweeping quality made possible by modern construction methods. We were soon shooting up through the corners, under a cloudless sky, blue and clear, with the mountains standing jagged and black, in contrast. Within minutes, my hunger was forgotten and I was fully focused on the simple joy of a perfect day on a motorbike. Just Sue had just regained her mountain legs when we rumbled out into the pass and pulled into the expanse of flat ground that formed a car park for the café. It was the sort of perfect morning that made me ignore my hunger for a while and wander around taking unnecessary photographs in the belief that these would somehow recreate the moment for Jo, a world away. Of course, this never works. The images, and my enthusiastic description, only had the effect of making her homesick for a mountain pass she had never visited and for her place on Team Elephant.

After breakfast, I took a last photo of an achingly blue sky over the Nufenen Glacier then fired Just Sue down the road to the west. This route allowed me to join the old road over the St Gotthard Pass from where I could loop back north through Andermatt, which was fast becoming my Swiss town of last resort. The St Gotthard is one of the oldest and most important passes in the Alps. My experience with crossbowman Tell had already revealed how important the Gotthard trade had been in the early establishment of the federation and the building of Lucerne. It also had a direct impact on the political reach of the new confederacy. In 1503, the Italian speaking area of Ticino on the southern end of the pass signed the Treaty of Arona and threw its lot in with the German-speaking Swiss.

The Gotthard had been known from antiquity but it was not an important crossing until the 13th century. Before then, travellers struggled to cross the fast-flowing Reuss River and the Schöllenen Gorge. Bridging the gorge was extraordinarily difficult for the engineers of the time and, unsurprisingly, the first bridge over the Schöllenen was called the Teufelsbrücke, or Devil's Bridge. The engineering effort to complete it could, the pundits said, only have been made with the aid of the devil. The original 13th century bridge is long gone and the road was realigned many times before the first rail tunnel was completed in 1882 at the cost of 197 lives. I joined the pass road on the Italian-speaking southern approach where the pass is known as the San Gottardo and they make a passable espresso. It was an easy ride to the top through a series of fast sweepers and a few lazy switchbacks. I turned around in the car park at the top and rode down the way I had come up, this time making some stops for photographs. A short search and a stop for directions at the bottom got me onto the 'old' road, known as the Tremola Road. Much of it was cobbled and it provided a much more interesting ride to the pass on the second ascent. Although, I might have been less enthusiastic had it been raining; riding a motorcycle, on wet cobbles would have been more excitement than I needed.

The pass itself was a dreary circus of food, produce and souvenir stalls with vehicles filling the limited number of close parks. Motorcycles were parked everywhere. There was a museum that provided some background on the Devil's Bridge (take the Tremola Road to see the site) and confirmation that the oldest record of the pass being named in honour of the Bavarian Saint Gotthard of Hildersheim was in 1236. I bought some mountain cheese and smoked beef sausage from a farmer's stall and found a place to eat lunch on the top of a large rock overlooking the scene. Vehicles were leaving and arriving constantly, the kebab stall was doing a roaring trade, the farmer sold a few more blocks of cheese, bikers stood around and yarned, and the little hatchbacks mewled around the edges of a cluster of tight-packed motor homes; just another pass in the mountains from what I could see.

What I did find interesting were the two monuments that took pride of place. The first was a pile dedicated to famous Swiss aviator Guex, who died in the Alps at a time when flying over the mountains was a lot more challenging. The monument was completed in 1928 by Fausto Agnelli and featured a number of large eagles, which seem to be watching the observer with a vulture's eye. The second is a rather beguiling bronze dedicated to Russian general Alexander Suvorov, who led a Russian campaign against the French in Italy. The bronze shows the slight, almost dainty, figure of Suvorov, on horseback and rugged against the cold, being led by a sturdy mountain type with a staff. At first I thought it was St Gotthard himself doing the right thing by a traveller, albeit one with an army, but it wasn't so. This was just a generic mountain man.

I drifted away to the north, taking a lazy roll down into the valley to intersect the Andermatt road and then turning west on the main road to ride back over the Furkapass, then north over Grimselpass and on towards Interlaken. I was sure I had been over Furkapass so many times that must know every pothole by name. I needed fuel and coffee and, for no particular reason, decided to make the stop at the village of Meiringen where I was amazed to find a statue of the fictional detective Sherlock Holmes in the main square. Anyone with one of those doorstop guidebooks on Switzerland would no doubt be surprised at my ignorance as I'm sure the village would be on a list of tourist must-visits. In my own defence I can only say that those books are too bulky to carry on the bike and it is much more fun to discover these places by chance.

The nearby Reichenbach Falls was the place in 1891 where Holmes was done in by the dastardly Professor Moriarty and the town has made something of a celebration of the fictional event. As well as the statue, the nearby Baker Street and Conan Doyle Place hardly have traditional names in this part of Switzerland. This discovery raised the obvious question about why Conan Doyle had selected this obscure place as the scene for the demise of his hero. It seemed a simple enough question at the time, but in answering it, I discovered another powerful force in the development of Switzerland and yet another English influence in the Alps.

Although the Victorian England of Conan Doyle was the pre-eminent industrial power, its wealth had come at a cost. The industrial cities were crowded, polluted and generally unhealthy places and in the wealthiest of nations, one in six of the population died of tuberculosis or consumption, as it was known at the time. Before the middle of the 19th century English and German doctors had noted that the prognosis for tuberculosis sufferers improved with exercise and fresh air. It didn't take long for a few enterprising medicos to declare that 'alpine air' was a cure. An German–Swiss doctor, Alexander Spengler, promoted Davos as a place where the locals were immune from the disease that ravaged the remainder of Europe. Throughout the 1860s the idea caught on with the medical establishment in both Europe and England, and Davos became the first of a number of 'cure stations' across the Alps. By 1877 the idea of the alpine cure had caught on, an invasion of the English infirm was underway, and the prosperous new industry of providing for them was enriching the Swiss.

Conan Doyle's wife suffered with tuberculosis and it was this that brought him to Davos in 1893. He spent the long winter devoted to his writing, writing the dramatic end of Holmes at the Reichenbach Falls. He also became an accomplished skier and an early pioneer of the sport. Conan Doyle was never a fan of his creation Sherlock Holmes and was pleased to be done with him. If you are a Sherlock Holmes buff it is worth a visit to Meiringen. The statue, created in 1988 by John Doubleday, has hidden in it clues to Holmes mysteries. I couldn't see any of them, but since I had never liked the crusty Holmes much this isn't surprising. The greatest mystery of all, however, is how the monument came to be erected by the 'Norwegian Explorers of Minnesota'. I have no idea what the Minnesota Norwegians were doing in Meiringen, but I'm sure the answer is there somewhere!

Despite all this mucking about I eventually got to Interlaken, which, as the name makes clear, occupies the ground between Thunnersee and the Brienzersee. It was a smart-looking town jammed full of summer tourists and traffic. There was nothing really wrong with the place but it just wasn't where I wanted to spend a couple of days. Another half hour coaxing Just Sue up a tortured road on the northern shore of Thunnersee found the little tourist village of Beatenberg and a comfortable room with an amazing view from its balcony. A thousand metres below, the colourful boats on the perfect mid-blue lake were so tiny I couldn't make out the crew. Looking directly across the lake at the mountains, three huge snow-covered peaks stood proud against a faded blue sky. The Eiger, the Mönch and the Jungfrau seemed so close I could almost reach out and touch them across the valley. Shortly after I came back onto the balcony to find the three peaks covered with cloud, a state they steadfastly maintained for the next two days. Cloud or not, these mountains made it difficult to look away. They seemed to change by the minute but were always mysterious and emitted a brutal energy that seemed threatening. It is not hard to understand that most of the high peaks of the Alps remained unclimbed well into the 19th century. Nor is it hard to accept the number of climbers who died on the early attempts.

It was the English once again who pioneered recreational climbing in the Alps. This was the period when a newly urbanised and prosperous English middle class was formulating the conduct of many group sports, setting down the rules of football, rugby, hockey and other modern games. The early alpinists, or cragsmen as they were sometimes known, took the same approach and formed The Alpine Club in London in 1857. Jim Ring summarises the club as a place where those Englishmen interested 'in the pursuit ... might meet their fellow enthusiasts, compare notes, discuss adventures, plan future expeditions and – in a high-minded age – contribute towards the advance of knowledge.'[11] The first meeting included the experienced alpinists of the day and the club quickly grew to a membership of more than one hundred and fifty. The membership was, by any measure, elite and included leading academics, clergymen, lawyers, diplomats and civil servants. But despite the nature of their careers (or perhaps because of it) they were the ones who made the first assaults on most of the high peaks of the Alps.

Included among the first members was John Murray, author and publisher of the 1852 *Alpine Handbook*, which was by then the standard text for alpine travellers. Quality publications became a feature of the club and, in 1859, the first of a series of pamphlets titled *Peaks, Passes and Glaciers* became generally available. A few years later, the club's official publication, *The Alpine Journal* was started. Alpine Club publications were of high quality and featured excellent writing as well as woodcuts, maps and colour printing. The tales of adventure and daring-do in the high Alps struck a chord with the imperial mindset of the time and there was a dramatic surge in interest in the new 'sport' of mountain climbing.

This period of amateur adventurers reached it zenith in the middle of the century but by 1900 was largely at an end. The accounts of the climbs from this period make remarkable reading. Often there was no useful preparation of the climbers and many of the expeditions were extravagantly provisioned. A large entourage would tote all the essential luxuries up the mountain behind the climbers and no expedition of this time would have been complete without sufficient wine and spirits to provide proper sustenance for the gentleman (and sometimes gentlewomen) climbers. Even tables and chairs were occasionally carted along so that a proper meal prepared by a cook could be enjoyed at the summit.

The American writer Mark Twain (Samuel Clemens) satirised these amateur expeditioners mercilessly in his classic travel tale *A Tramp Abroad*. Twain simply describes his own, totally fictional, expedition. His assault on the excesses, however, is merciless.

'The expedition consists of 198 persons, including the mules; or 205, including the cows. As follows: Myself 1 Veterinary Surgeon Mr Harris 1 Butler 17 Guides 12 Waiters 4 Surgeons 1 Footman 1 Geologist 1 Barber 1 Botanist 1 Head Cook 3 Chaplains 9 Assistants 2 Draftsman 4 Pastry Cooks 15 Barkeepers 1 Confectionery Artist 1 Latinist.'[12]

The list goes on to become more and more absurd and includes such essentials as 143 pairs of crutches, 22 barrels of whiskey and 154 umbrellas. Like all good satire, Twain's contains a core of truth. Many expeditions were woefully ill-prepared for the mountains with sometimes tragic consequences. The seriousness of this hit the wider public in 1865 when a poorly trained and equipped expedition to the summit of the Matterhorn, led by the famous alpinist Edward Whymper, went wrong. The party had reached the summit of the mountain but on the descent, four climbers fell to their deaths. The severed rope that saved the survivors from being pulled to their deaths with the fallen climbers is on display in Zermatt's Alpine Museum. One of the fatalities was minor English nobility and the others were from well-connected families. This assured the most graphic coverage of the incident in London, followed by an investigation and years of claims and counter-claims of what had gone wrong from those left alive.

While the Matterhorn tragedy was being played out in London and in the French courts, well-prepared and professional European climbers started to arrive in the Alps and, within a few years, the nature of the sport had changed and the influence of the Alpine Club's members had diminished. By 1900, it was no longer appropriate to carry sufficient bottles of wine on a climb to ensure that meals were taken in a civilised fashion.

Beatenberg was a spectacular place for a couple of rest days but, like a lot of smaller Swiss tourist villages on our route, it had seen better days. There were several hotels and many businesses closed up and the place looked in need of some basic maintenance. The owner of the small restaurant where I had dinner was pessimistic. The problem was simple enough. The high value of the Swiss Franc against the Euro had made Switzerland prohibitively expensive for the working-class Europeans who had made up the clientele of the cheaper resorts. The top end of the market was probably doing well, she opined, but the tradition of having a family holiday in the Alps had been replaced with more exotic adventures at the end of a cheap flight. By the time I had paid the bill and started an idle stroll back to my digs I knew what she meant. A simple meal of sausages and potatoes with a local wine and a strudel dessert had set me back the equivalent of US$50!

After Beatenberg, the backroads took Just Sue south-west through Gstaad and over Col du Pillon and Col du Croix and on to the ski resort of Villars-sur-Ollon, which in the summer was used for tramping, mountain biking and watching sunsets with a glass of over-chilled chardonnay. I found the small comfortable apartment near the centre of town, lent to us by a friend so that Team Elephant could re-group and recover from a few hectic weeks. As I lugged the bags up a few flights of stairs I was very pleased not to be moving on for a while. The next day I rode down to the airport and sat waiting in the terminal for the Thursday 0950 flight from Frankfurt. Jo appeared on cue, with a cheeky smile and the practised nonchalance that only comes from experience. I handed her the pants from her riding suit.

'You might want to change into these', I said. 'We've got some riding to do and we need to get moving.' The best crew in the world gave a short laugh. It was great to have the team back together. That night I noted in my journal that the pick-up had gone well and that we were now 'good at this sort of thing'. It was strange what we had become good at in life.

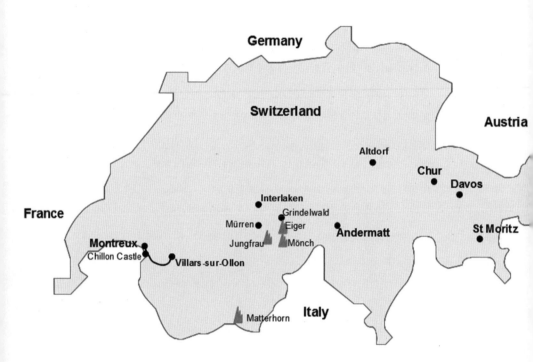

Germany

Switzerland

Austria

France

Altdorf

Chur

Davos

Interlaken

Grindelwald

Mürren

Eiger

Andermatt

St Moritz

Jungfrau

Mönch

Montreux

Chillon Castle

Villars-sur-Ollon

Matterhorn

Italy

8

THE ALPS AND THE MAKING OF MODERN SWITZERLAND

Villars-sur-Ollon was certainly not the sort of swept-up resort we would usually choose for a week off. Like a lot of specialist ski resorts it was expensive even by Swiss standards. Its great advantage to us was the free use of a friend's apartment and the chance to rest and do our own cooking for a while. The place was small but comfortable and located in the middle of town right next to the cog railway to the ski fields. The little train wound its way up and back all day with walkers and mountain bikers and downhill scooter riders. The hills around the town were busy with summer sports and the bars and restaurants were doing a brisk trade.

It was a short train ride up to the ski lift, which seemed to be doing good business in the summer delivering folk engaged in all manner of mountain sports to a start point high above the village. There were walkers of every calibre, from family groups out for a short stroll in the meadows to the serious and well-equipped groups starting a longer tramp to the next valley or beyond. Further up, rock climbers were studying their climbing guides and looking for an excuse to start while another group was busy with hang gliders of one type or another. There were also plenty of mountain bikers taking the easy way up so they could take the fast way down, but a group we had never seen before were the downhill scooter riders. These folk were equipped with bizarre adult-size scooters similar to the old-fashioned pneumatic wheel ones we rode as kids, except these were equipped with knobby balloon tyres and tiny disc brakes. The idea was simple, take the ski lift up, ride the scooter down the track back to the village as fast as you dared then return to the top and do it all again. It was not just all mad physical activity in the hills. There were also anglers trying their luck in the tiny mountain lakes, twitchers looking for bird sightings and photographers kneeling over wild flowers with short-focus lenses. In short, the mountains around Villars were busy, very busy.

Villars is also home to several exclusive private schools, one of which is, by reputation, the most expensive in Switzerland. Although it was summer holidays, there seemed to be plenty of pupils in residence, who were filling their days with a program of sports and activities. Interestingly, the town also had a substantial ex-patriot community as it was in one of the few cantons that allowed non-Swiss citizens to buy and own property. These part-time owners had pushed the villa-sprawl over a substantial area and, no doubt, locked in a useful tax intake for the city burghers. In a clear demonstration of the financial security of the town, a round of the European show-jumping championship was held each year. The arena was shoehorned into a tiny parcel of flat ground clinging to the hillside. It was hardly a good site for the competitors, but I suspect the competitors were not the reason it was held in Villars.

All of this made Villars one of the most expensive places we had ever stayed. One day I decided to cook a special meal for some minor celebration and walked to the local butcher. I surveyed the meat on display and decided the veal looked good and the price per kilo was acceptable, if not reasonable. The butcher finished serving another customer and it was then that I noticed the small print on the price tag. The price was for 100g of meat. I must have looked a bit stunned as I did the mental arithmetic to multiply by 10 then convert the result from Swiss Francs to dollars. The veal was well over US$80 per kilo. I felt my face flush as I asked for a kilo of chicken thighs, which were slapped down on the counter with the bad grace of a shopkeeper deprived of a good sale. From then on our shopping was done down in the industrial town in the valley and the village shops were left for a few emergency buys and some fresh bread.

Walking the hills around the town and observing the variety of mountain adventurers, you could still feel the awe in which the mountains were held. Clearly, somewhere between Professor Scheucher's dragon-fearing 18th century and the Alps-worshipping 21st century there had been a substantial turn around in attitude. The Alps had captured the popular imagination and these days the mountains are considered by many as a spiritual place where you can commune with nature, be close to God ... or something like that. I take a more pragmatic view of mountains, borne of good army training as a young National Service soldier more than 40 years ago. I always look at the hills and imagine a week walking uphill with 40kg of equipment. It brings back long forgotten memories of searing pain and tends to kill the mountain romance stone dead.

In the mid-20th century, the popular view of the mountains, already hijacked by Johanna Spyri's much-filmed *Heidi*, reached a syrupy zenith with the film *The Sound of Music*. Released in 1965, the Rodgers and Hammerstein musical tells the story of the von Trapp family who escape from Nazi Austria over the mountains to Italy. The screenplay and a Broadway version were based on a 1949 memoir by Maria von Trapp. The Maria of the movie starts the story as the children's governess and ends as Mrs von Trapp providing the necessarily satisfying romantic ending. After 40 years, the movie still has a cult following, due mainly to a quality musical score and the singing of the female lead, Julie Andrews. The real-life Trapps eventually made their way to the United States, but did so via Switzerland, not Italy, and set up in show business as the Trapp Family Singers. These days, the Trapp Family Lodge still trades in Stowe, Vermont, and includes in its program Music in the Meadow, a concert where the current generation reprise all the Rodgers and Hammerstein favourites.

While the movie is only vaguely connected to the real events of that traumatic time, it continued a trend for a modern idealisation of the Alps. The Nazis are the film's evil-doers and, as we discovered in Berchtesgaden, the Nazis were fascinated by the Alps. For the Nazis, the Alps were about rugged beauty and Aryan heroism, a place where men triumphed against nature.

This heroic view of the mountains was idealised in films. In a series of popular mountain movies, shot mainly in the 1920s, the German director, Arnold Fanck provided the first quality production for the genre and gave a starring role to Leni Riefenstahl. Riefenstahl later moved from acting to film-making and became a favourite of Hitler. She went on to chronicle the rise of the Nazi party and produced a number of noted propaganda films. Fanck's man-against-mountain classics, however, stand up well in their own right and are still film festival regulars.

But 20th century artistic alpinists like Fanck and Riefenstahl were merely the most recent in a line of writers and artists who had rehabilitated the mountains in the public mind. The saccharin sweet Heidi and Maria and the buffed heroes of the Third Reich were building on a romantic foundation that began more than 100 years before when the first influential travellers returned from the mountains with exotic tales. Among the alpine tourists in first wave was the Genevan philosopher and writer Jean-Jacques Rousseau whose *Discourse on the Origin of Inequality* influenced the French Revolution, the United States' Founding Fathers, and modern political thought. Like other Enlightenment thinkers, Rousseau was a polymath and it was his autobiography and one of his novels that were influential in changing the way Europe's elite viewed the Alps.

Rousseau's *Confessions* is a very modern autobiography: 'To fall at the feet of an imperious mistress, obey her mandates, or implore pardon, were for me the most exquisite enjoyments, and ...'—well, you get the idea. The work is modern mostly in its self-absorption. It provides only a limited account of the years Rousseau spent in the service of his benefactor Madame de Warens, near Annecy in the French Alps, which is where he found such a sympathetic eye for the mountains themselves. That interest was given full flight in the novel *La Nouvelle Héloïse*, released in 1761, which was an immediate success. It was printed in 72 authorised French editions by 1800 and, with no copyright laws, in numerous counterfeit editions. The first English edition was also printed in 1761, which is a good indication of the speed with which ideas flowed across the Channel in those days. The novel was highly influential and more than a little controversial. This prompted the Catholic Church to place the work on its List of Prohibited Books—always a good way to ensure wide readership!

Before *La Nouvelle Héloïse*, outside nature played only a small part in 18th-century literature. After its publication, the portrayal of nature became central to the novel. Rousseau uses nature to refer to the simplicity of the rustic life in the country as opposed to the corrupt life of the city. In this sense, nature has a moral element reflecting an Enlightenment attitude to the strictures of the churches of the time. The reader is left to consider the lovers at the centre of the story innocent despite their condemnation by the church. It was heady stuff and it is no wonder the novel struck a chord with a wide readership.

After a couple of days recovering in Villars, we found our way down to Montreux for lunch beside Lake Geneva. On the way, we made a stop at Chillon Castle to fill in a little more of this story. The castle juts out into the lake a few kilometres east of Montreux and had been the seat of power of the counts of Savoy from the 12th century. The place is now a popular tourist attraction, so much so that parking anywhere nearby is a problem, unless you are on a motorcycle of course. The tour was interesting, if not spectacular. The castle is neither opulent nor of great martial merit but it had one feature which captured our attention: the dungeon, which is genuinely dank and uncomfortable, was the place where François de Bonivard was imprisoned from 1530 to 1536.

De Bonivard was Prior of a monastery outside Geneva and fell into a dispute with the House of Savoy when he sided with the local burghers against increased Savoy influence in the region. He had been imprisoned between 1519 and 1521 when the majority of his land had been confiscated. He returned to the monastery in 1527 unrepentant and ended up in the cellar of Chillon for his trouble. He still had time on his release to marry four times, the last to an unfrocked nun, Catherine de Courtaronel, who was later arrested for immorality and infidelity and executed by drowning in the Rhône River.

François de Bonivard's imprisonment in Chillon Castle might have been lost in the wash of history except it captured the imagination of the English poet George Gordon (Lord Byron) and another minor English aristocrat named Percy Shelley. The two had met in Switzerland in 1816 and made a pilgrimage to see the wretched place for themselves. Byron famously engraved his name into the stone pillar to which Bonivard had been chained, then penned an epic poem: *The Prisoner of Chillon*. Of these, it is certainly the graffiti that has aged the better!

Neither Byron nor Shelley had gone all the way to Switzerland just to reflect on the memory of Bonivard, far from it. A short and unfortunate marriage, a troublesome mistress, unpaid debts and the interest of the bailiffs were all that were needed to recommend a long stay abroad for Byron. Shelley was escaping a failed marriage and was travelling with his new mistress, Mary Wollstonecraft. Both he and Byron, however, had certainly read and been influenced by Rousseau's Confessions and La Nouvelle Héloïse and continued the romanticising of the Alps. They were both celebrities back in London and their highly charged and romantic view of the Alps had a dramatic effect on the London elite. Mary Wollstonecraft eventually became Mary Shelley and made a solid contribution of her own with the novel *Frankenstein* written during the group's extended stay in Switzerland. While the novel ends in the snowdrifts of Siberia, it starts with a crazy doctor from Geneva and has its own share of 'Alp-y' romanticism.

The Chillon Castle we visited, with its crowds of tourists and safety railings, didn't seem threatening at all, but it was not a stretch to imagine how dark and unbearable the place would have been on a long winter's night. The prison space where Bonivard and others were kept is among the foundations piers of the castle, with the floor nothing more than the uneven bedrock itself. Even on a bright sunny day the high window let just a little light fall on the centre of the room away from the pillars where the inmates were chained. Byron's famous graffiti had, disappointingly, been covered with clear plastic to the frustration of the hordes of flash camera users. It seemed to us that the scratched signature was the main prize of the castle as the curious crouched low trying to make out the famous name. Fearing injury, I stood back and accepted that the mark was Byron's, as claimed.

Artists were also among those who rehabilitated the Alps. The great British landscape painter J. M. W. Turner is regarded as the artist who elevated landscape painting to an appreciation rivalling other popular forms. One of his early works, *Hannibal and his Army Crossing the Alps*, was one of the first paintings to portrait a wild and untamed nature as part of the central drama of the picture and one of the first to show the power of the mountains. It was a form pioneered by Turner and reflected a significant change in style. Most will have seen the famous painting by French artist Jacques-Louis David of Napoleon crossing the Alps, painted in 1801. The picture is dominated by Napoleon mounted on a white charger rearing on its hind legs on a rocky outcrop, which would have been a very dangerous manoeuvre on a mountain pass—so dangerous that Napoleon rode a sure-footed mule when he crossed the Great St Bernard Pass on his way to war with Austria. There is no doubt about the subject of David's painting. Napoleon dominates the canvas and nature is the background. Turner's Hannibal work was painted in 1812 but reflects a new way of seeing the mountains. Hannibal's army are tiny figures dwarfed by the mountains and the overbearing angry sky. Hannibal and his elephants are struggling against the wild mountains and it is nature that is the star of the picture. The men and beasts are insignificant. The shift from the neo-classicist David to the romanticist Turner reflected a new and dramatically different way of seeing the Alps and it caused a stir.

The impact of Turner's work was greatly amplified by the art critic John Ruskin, who was himself a lover of the Alps. Ruskin's leverage, however, was more dramatic than the title critic might imply. He was a polymath and one of the leading public intellectuals of the 19th century whose writings on art, politics and social organisation were all influential. So much so that Ruskinites formed utopian socialist colonies in Ruskin, Florida; Ruskin, British Columbia; and Dickson County, Tennessee. As late as 1918 there were still several hundred Ruskinites living in Ruskin, Florida. Clearly, Ruskin had an audience and his appraisal of Turner and lauding of alpine landscape had a dramatic affect on the way the intelligentsia saw the Alps. Interestingly, like Rousseau a century before, Ruskin didn't actually climb any mountains, nor did he like being on them. In his view, their beauty was best appreciated from afar, or better still, through the work of Turner.

Fortunately others were less squeamish about the climb and painters and alpinists followed in such large numbers that the Alps started to feel crowded. The romance of the Alps started to drift into the consciousness of a wider cross-section of society. With that new sensibility as a guide, an increasingly affluent middle class set out to see the mountains for themselves. While the English came first and in the largest numbers, they weren't alone in the mountains. Wealthy Germans and Americans were also there in numbers. Many recorded their experience in gushing language creating a new publishing genre. Judging by the number of titles produced, the accounts of those early travellers were widely read. Some, like the American writer Mark Twain made a fine job of it, mixing fiction and documentary and binding it all together with a gentle satire. In a typical Twain observation from *A Tramp Abroad*, he notes the early start in one village:

'We did not oversleep at St Nicholas. The church-bell began to ring at four-thirty in the morning, and from the length of time it continued to ring I judged that it takes the Swiss sinner a good while to get the invitation through his head.'[13]

Others, unfortunately, wrote turgid and self-important journals of the privileged class. By the middle of the 19th century, with Europe relatively free of major war for a period, the English invasion of the Alps was underway. Mass tourism had been invented and Switzerland became the first country to be marketed as a tourist 'destination'. It was a lucrative business and the Swiss prospered.

We had a chance to consider all of this over a late, ordinary and expensive Montreux lunch. Montreux was a stretched-out strip of a town clinging to the shore of Lake Geneva—clean, neat and well ordered. We chose a restaurant overlooking both the lake and a larger-than-life statue of the singer Freddie Mercury who had lived in Montreux. Judging by the dozens of tourists who were lining up to have their photograph taken under the three-metre high Freddie, there has been no let-up in the numbers of people keen to see for themselves what all the Alps fuss is about. People-watching is always good fun in these places. That day the jostling tourists were the newly wealthy Chinese middle class with a good smattering of Russians and Central and East Asians.

The mix has always been changing and the observations of the early tourists about each other are as interesting as their gushing descriptions of the scenery. Mark Twain famously mocks his countryman tourists and was critical of tourists in general, but did so with his usual acerbic and entertaining wit. Others simply reflected the prejudices of their class and background. An 1875 traveller, George Waring, from New York, between advising the Italians on how to run their railways and complimenting the breeding of the upper-class Germans, managed a swipe at the English 'whose ceaseless self-consciousness is an oppression to all about them'.[14] Then in a stunning demonstration of class snobbery run amok in the New World, describes the table manners of the locals:

'Among the coarser and uncultured of every society we expect little deference to the requirements of delicacy. But to see a pretty, dainty, tastefully dressed, sweet-looking young woman bearing both elbows hard on the table, stabbing her meat with a backhand blow with a fork, twisting her wrist and lowering her mouth to a convenient pitching distance, with the alternative by-play of a knife-blade charged with softer viands, produces a shock which no familiarity can soften. Only yesterday I saw a mild-eyed bride thus engaged, with the occasional interpolation of a pickled onion by her fond and admiring husband's deft harpoon. The effect was heightened by her quaffing a full litre of beer during the meal.'[15]

Whatever the travellers thought of each other, the tourist business expanded through the second half of the 19th century but remained a largely summer trade. It was not until the last decade of that century that winter sports started to drive a new and lucrative alpine economy. This may seem a little late as the first alpine ski club had been established in 1861 in Kiandra, Australia, where there is little snow and no mountains worthy of the name. When an Englishman named Henry Lunn took an interest in winter sports, things stated to happen for the Swiss. Lund had first gone to the Alps in 1892 as a Methodist minister to attend a church meeting at Grindelwald at the foot of the Eiger. He was fascinated by winter sports and the outdoors lifestyle. Skiing was by no measure a new activity in the 19th century. Everywhere there was regular snow, people had always travelled on skis because it was recognised as the easiest and quickest way to move over the snow. What Lund brought with him was an Englishman's love of sport for its own sake and an eye for a good business opportunity. Lunn established the Public Schools Alpine Sports Club and by the early years of the 20th century package ski holidays, complete with instruction, were being conducted. The club also started a notion of exclusivity that has lingered around skiing ever since. It was limited to ex-public schoolboys, alumni of the older universities and those holding the Queen's Commission in the Services.

Many of those commissioned officers had returned from India and had taken up the new sport of skiing while serving on the North-West Frontier. A group of officers founded a downhill racing club and an event called the Roberts of Kandahar Cup, which is claimed by some to be the oldest downhill ski race. It wasn't long before the name Kandahar was being applied to a number of downhill races, establishing a little-known link between Switzerland and Afghanistan. The Roberts in question was Field Marshall Frederick Sleigh Roberts, 1st Earl Roberts, who in 1878 led an army in the Second Afghan War.

Lunn's son Arnold grew up in the fledgling skiing industry and took over the ski empire based at Mürren. Arnold Lunn made a substantial contribution to the development of the sport in his own right. He wrote the rules for downhill skiing, staged the first slalom in 1922 and the first world championship in 1931. Interestingly, it was the Englishman Arnold Lunn who persuaded the Olympics organisation to accept downhill and slalom skiing as a sport. I say interesting because the English had no tradition of alpine sports and have never had much success at them. The proposal was also vigorously opposed by the Scandinavian countries, who were committed to the tradition of cross-country skiing and ski jumping. Lunn, however, prevailed and the sport of going up a mountain just so you can ski down it was launched. The curious traveller can visit a garden next to the railway station in the picture-postcard village of Mürren and find a plaque commemorating Sir Arnold Lunn's achievements and note with satisfaction that his contribution was recognised with a knighthood at home and is remembered by the Swiss.

The elitism of the English ski industry was reflected in all of the other areas of English influence and caused a degree of friction. Upper-class English were horrified to hear Cockney accents in the Alps and thought their presence reflected badly on England. Once middle-class ski packages were underway, the Public Schools Alpine Sports Club started to book whole hotels so that its members wouldn't have to mix with the riff-raff. The newcomers were considered vulgar. But as Jim Ring points out: 'Vulgar though some may have considered them, such travellers had arrived; and vulgar or not, they would continue to come.'[16] In a broader sense, the English, regardless of class, remained amazingly impervious to the various alpine Europeans. They shunned most aspects of alpine life and created a further lucrative industry importing their preferred food and facilities from home. The locals got on with the job of learning English, making a good trade importing English specialities and mastered the art of overcharging their guests for the privilege of insularity.

The behaviour of the tourists did not pass without comment and many at the time were vocal about the pernicious effect the unrestrained foreigners were having on the place. One of the most vocal and most effective critics was John Ruskin who famously described 'a consuming white leprosy of new hotels'. Whatever their faults, however, the visitors brought a new economy, which changed the country and established a basis of Swiss prosperity. Considering the abject poverty that marked alpine life at the end of the 18th century, the change had been dramatic. Things were going well, and continued to go well until the assassination of a minor royal in Sarajevo in 1914 sparked a cataclysmic world war.

The Swiss had clung tenaciously to their ideal of armed neutrality and structured their defence around an armed militia, but this was an idea that had run its course by World War I. They nonetheless manned the barricades and the male population spent the war years rotating between the trenches and the economy, while the belligerents slugged it out 800km to the north. At the end of the fighting, Switzerland had been spared simply because there was no useful military reason to go there. It was, however, so affected by the conflict that in 1920 it abandoned its long-held tradition of neutrality and joined the other nations of the world in the newly formed League of Nations. The Swiss flirtation with collective security did not last long. The League's mishandling of the Italian invasion of Abyssinia was sufficient for the Swiss to realise there would be no collective security and the notion of armed neutrality was revived.

The Swiss survival in World War I gave strength to the myth of Switzerland as an armed mountain fortress, at least for those who had never studied a map. For the rest, including, one presumes, the German High Command, Swiss vulnerability was obvious. While the Alps comprised about 60 per cent of Switzerland, a relatively small part of the 8 million Swiss lived and worked there. Most Swiss lived on the plateau where the important cities of Zurich and Geneva are located. These areas are given little protection by the Alps and are easily accessible from the Rhône Valley to the west or over the rolling plateau from Germany.

The myth of the mountain fortress and the late revival of the doctrine of armed neutrality left the Swiss poorly prepared for another war. The historian Angelo Codevilla found that the Swiss 'ground forces were not equipped for modern warfare. Each battalion had only one infantry cannon that could be used against tanks, plus just two grenade launchers.'[17] The strategy was to fight a defensive battle from prepared positions and launch counterattacks, some with horse cavalry. But, '...the first news of the German campaign in Poland showed all this to be a pipe dream.'[18] With the collapse of France, Swiss neutrality was vulnerable and its defence rested on a calculation that the economy was 'worth more alive than dead'. The Swiss spent the remainder of the war balancing the demands the Allies and the Axis both of which blockaded the country.[19]

The level of Swiss cooperation waxed and waned with the fortunes of the combatants. Both sides used the Swiss currency for exchange purposes, at vastly different rates depending on which side had the ascendency. Both sides were able to access essential materials from the other through Switzerland. Both sides used threats and intimidation in the bargaining. It became fashionable in the 1990s to claim that the Swiss had cooperated too much with the Nazis and not enough with the Allies, but this assertion doesn't stand up to scrutiny. The Allies were not in a position to invade if they couldn't get what they needed any other way. The Nazis certainly were and certainly would have done so. Despite this, Codevilla notes that the Swiss government went to extraordinary lengths to track down and weed out (sometimes by execution) Nazi sympathisers. At the end of the war, Churchill was fulsome in his praise for the way the Swiss had behaved and thought Swiss sympathy for the Allies more impressive considering the German heritage of the majority of Swiss.

These discoveries bring us full circle to modern Switzerland and to the realisation that there is something in the Swiss character that draws deeply on the Alps. The legend of Tell, the importance of Rütli Meadow and the long gestation of a unique form of Swiss government have made the Swiss a unique alpine people somehow different from those of their linguistic homelands. Rub along with any Swiss for a while and you realise that the spirit of the foundational myths runs deep and that here is a people deeply committed to their Swiss identity. As it was explained to me, a French Swiss, a German Swiss or an Italian Swiss can all walk tall with a full measure of ownership of their proud Swiss identity. As French, Germans or Italians they would always be on the fringe, alpine bumpkins, always less than the elites at the centre of those countries.

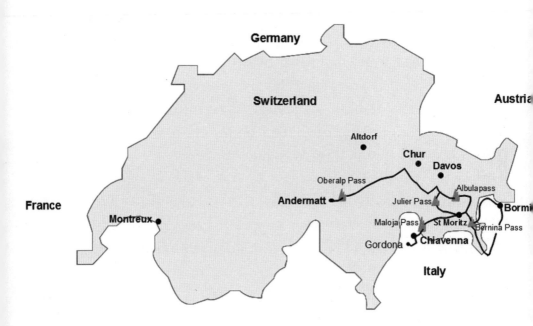

9

THE ITALIAN ALPS

By the end of our time in Villars-sur-Ollon, we were well rested and thankful for our extended break. Jo had spend an exhausting couple of weeks getting to the other side of the world, seeing to her mother's funeral and the associated administration, and getting back to Alps. And, although these weeks were not as difficult for me and Just Sue, it wasn't all beer and skittles for us. Well, actually, there was quite a lot of beer now I think of it ... but definitely no skittles.

After dropping Jo in Munich, my meandering route eventually landed me in Andermatt, well positioned for explorations to both the east and west. Before heading west through the centre of Switzerland, I made a broad sweep to the east and south to cross important passes to Italy and explore the Italian alpine regions. This part of the route was poorly planned without Jo at work on the research and I had done no more than mark some key passes on the maps and mark out a route with a highlighter. East from Andermatt across the Oberalppass on the Chur road, I turned off south towards St Moritz, then east again towards Davos, then south again over the Albulapass. Off the main roads at last, I let Just Sue get some healthy exercise and for much of the ride from the north, we followed the Rhaetian Railway, which crossed the road on some impressive stone viaducts. The railway, built in 1903, disappeared into a 5.9km tunnel well short of the pass, then reappeared on the southern side away from the road.

The road up to the pass was rough, pot-holed and narrow. So narrow that passing a car was impossible, or at least very dangerous, unless the car cooperated by moving over in the occasional wider section of road. Unfortunately, my journey coincided with that of a classic sports car club. There were about a dozen cars all built in the 1950s or 1960s, most of them wandering along in a daze at such a low speed I needed to slip Just Sue's clutch on some switchbacks. It wasn't that they were travelling so slowly that caused my aggravation. Rather, it was that they seemed completely oblivious to the drivers behind who weren't quite so relaxed. For my part, I gently nudged Just Sue past one car after another generally slipping around the outside in a tight corner where there was plenty of visibility. Most drivers in the Alps are very considerate and make room as soon as it is safe to do so. These cars, however, were on a touring holiday and clearly didn't know, or didn't care about, the usual rules. They were too busy talking and pointing out the scenery to notice what was behind.

The Albula was not one of the great pass roads but it had a good variety of easy and tight curves and a little café at the top. I had read on a biker's blog that marmots were readily seen from the café deck but it was marmot free that day. As the temperature was up over 30°C in the valleys the smart marmots were probably staying underground in the cool. What did turn up, however, was a stag. Well, it didn't actually turn up. It was driven up, its head and mighty antlers hanging over the back of a small trailer being pulled by a smaller car. The hunters pulled up outside the café and stood proudly by their kill enjoying a beer while everyone in the area came up and examined the body and declared it the finest they had seen in many years. The hunters were bursting with pride while they posed at the back of the trailer with their rifles, holding the points between them.

Hunters are common in the Alps, particularly the French Alps, and particularly on Sunday. They are often dressed in elaborate camouflage clothing, no doubt to help them stalk a wary prey, but also wear a high visibility vest over their camouflage duds. In France at least, this is a legal requirement to try to limit the number of hunters who bag each other instead of the game. I am sure that most only go 50m into the undergrowth before removing the vests but they still made an amusing sight standing in small groups with their dogs and 4×4s by the road. My other observation of the Sunday hunters is that the ones who turned up with the stag were unusual. They looked like fit, tough mountain men. Most hunters we saw were too soft-looking to do any serious tracking and stalking in those steep places.

I did plenty of hunting when I was growing up and I remember those expeditions with some affection. They were among the few things that I ever did with my father and those adventures gave me my first opportunity to talk to him man to man. Many of the simple things I learned from those long cold nights have guided me well through a life more complex than he could have ever imagined. These days, however, I am not a fan of hunting and don't think well of those who do it. I put the change down to my time as a conscript soldier more than 40 years ago. The Infantry taught me how to do it properly and that the only time it is a test of anything worthwhile is when the hunted shoot back.

I downed my Albula Pass coffee without ceremony, left the hunters to it and pressed on. With the sports cars all parked back at the café, the road was reasonably clear and if the track south was rough this was a small price for such a picturesque ride. This route also allowed me to continue to the Bernina Pass then turn north on the back roads and cross into Italy and the town of Bormio. We had reached Bormio some weeks earlier from the north over the Stelvio Pass. If all this twisting and turning seems a little aimless, there was now a little logic in the route selection that might not be obvious. Switzerland has two distinctive features that impacted on our planning. First, it is very a very expensive country. Second, it is a very small country. Taking these characteristics at face value, it was useful to be out of Switzerland by the end of the travelling day, which provided a notable benefit to a meagre budget. The side benefit of this was staying at some smaller and lesser-known places and making some interesting discoveries. Not that Bormio was a good choice for an out-of-the-way stop. The town was a modern ski resort and had been a spa town since Roman times. It had an expensive look and feel to it, but off-season there was plenty of cheap modest accommodation available. It also allowed an easy loop to cross back into Switzerland over the Bernina Pass from the southern side.

I thought the Bernina was a pleasant ride, but I was getting used to high passes by then and I was harder to impress than I had been. The Italian loop brought me back to Switzerland and onto the main valley road where I turned left towards St Moritz and an even more glitzy resort. St Moritz and Davos are at one end of the ski business. While Mürren may have the special honour of being the place where modern skiing started, it had evolved into a nice family sort of place. These two towns, however, had turned it into a money-making machine. St Moritz is a glittering jewel of a town stretched around the northern and western sides of Lake St Moritz. The place is squeaky clean, well ordered and very organised. Even on a motorcycle there were few places to park without parting with some Swiss Francs and there were plenty of people keen to enforce the rules. There were manicured parks and walkways by the lake, smart shops, trendy cafes and swept-up restaurants. This was the quintessential holiday town trying hard to cater for everyone. The accommodation matched its ambition with not-too-ugly apartment blocks at one level, the most exclusive chalets at the other and plenty of variety in between. Over a coffee I was considering staying for a couple of days and just hanging out by the lake hoping the weather would cool. But, when I got the 20 Swiss Franc bill for a small tart and a coffee, I thought better of it, pulled my sweat-soaked jacket back on and rolled out of town to the south-west. It turned out to be a good move.

The road back towards Italy was an easy ride along the northern bank of Silvaplanasee and Silsersee, but a little beyond that it simply dropped away into the valley in front of me. The Maloja Pass plummeted down from the plateau and into the Valtelline Valley. Two corners into the descent Just Sue had her balance and we were off down the valley wall like a runaway train. About halfway down I closed on a large rigid truck dragging a low gear. As I slowed I glanced over the side to the road below to see a second truck on its way up and calculated that the two would arrive at the hairpin bend just ahead at about the same time. Remembering the old advice to stand well clear of mating elephants, I pulled Just Sue into the side, grabbed the camera from the tank bag and found a vantage point to watch the action. To my surprise, both trucks entered the corner at the same time then slowed and started to jockey back and forth for position. In a series of see-sawing manoeuvres each inched past the other as though choreographed and practised. Within a few minutes the trucks were through and the few cars waiting patiently back from the corner were on their way. Clearly they have done all this before!

The road flattened and straightened on the valley floor but the pass had been such an unexpected delight that I turned Just Sue around and rode up and down again because, well, just because I could. By the time I was back on the valley floor for the second time, it was the middle of the day and very hot. Half an hour later when the pass road had delivered me into the town of Chiavenna, the last cool of the high plateau had been replaced with a stifling valley humidity, and I was soaked through with sweat and feeling dehydrated. Had Jo been with me I would have suggested we call it a day, find some digs and get out of the heat. But on my own, I felt strangely guilty about stopping early and decided to have a lunch break and press on.

I made a quick pass through town, found a place to park across from the railway station and started towards the railway café looking for a quick snack. A few steps inside the door of the old stone building I stopped and let my eyes adjust to the light. An animated ruckus had formed by the ticket window.

There was a dispute. Excited arms beat air into slow waves I could taste, wet on my lips. To the right, the café, separated by a shimmering opaque shaft of light from a high window, held the fuzzy outline of full chairs and a funk of smoke. A single drop of sweat made a languid descent from my brow, hung for a moment on the tip of my nose then dropped silently on the dusty floor. I turned towards the tourist desk in the corner.

'I need a room for tonight. Cheap. Comfortable.'

'If you don't mind being a few kilometres out of town there is a good place in a little village.'

'How far?'

'A few kilometres.'

A raised eyebrow.

'Not more than 10.'

A nod of acceptance, a few minutes programming the GPS, a hasty thanks and I was outside looking up into a fierce blue sky taking deep breaths of the searing air.

The pension was at the top of a tangle of village named Gordona high on the western wall of the valley eight kilometres from Chiavenna and easily found thanks largely to the GPS. I stopped in the street, switched off the engine, took of my helmet and climbed down. An old woman was sitting in an ancient straight-backed chair in a shaded doorway. I smiled respectfully, *buongiorno nonna*. The old woman smiled back and pointed up the street. Maria walked towards me, purposeful and handsome with a ring of keys and an easy smile. The upstairs apartment had two bedrooms, a nice bathroom, a kitchen and a large living area. A balcony stared south into the summer haze towards Lake Como, the valley side tumbling down into an out of focus drab shimmer. Maria gave me a detailed brief on the apartment and the area's attractions in Italian. I understood nothing but nodded and said si at the appropriate junctures. Then, while she was busy explaining something of vital importance about the refrigerator, I noticed a framed photo on the wall. When I looked closely it was of Maria, with a man I took to be her husband, both in riding leathers, posed around a shiny Moto Guzzi by the Arctic Circle marker in Norway.

I let out an exclamation and we both stood there grinning and smiling at the recognition that we were not strangers after all but lost members of a common tribe and that we did, indeed, have a common language. I explained that Jo was travelling with me but had to return home for her mother's funeral and that she would rejoin me soon and gave Maria the link to our website. We spent a few minutes recounting some of our moto-experiences, in Italian or English, both somehow easily understood. Finally she asked a question which I took to be about dinner. We had a short conversation which ended with 7pm, then Maria was gone. I stripped off and took a long cold shower, washed my riding suit, found a cold beer in the fridge and tested it against my cheek. It was European cold. I put it into the freezer to get seriously cold and made a note in my journal to buy a replacement, then settled down in the shade of an open doorway where the breeze might cool my naked skin.

By the time 7pm rolled around, the sun had dropped below the mountains and left the valley in a smoky twilight with the headlights on the valley road standing out through the haze. The cool of the evening was still a few hours away but I was showered, changed, refreshed and idly curious about the night ahead. Right on time there was a knock and a huge grin, followed by a woolly head, appearing around the open door. Roberto spoke no English but was fluent in motorcycle, especially the local dialect known as Moto Guzzi. We had a thoughtful inspection of Just Sue then clambered into his little car to roll down the hill through the maze of streets to a bar just off the main road. There was plenty of parking space outside but few cars. Inside we found the owner Giandomenico and his father Marcello watching over an impressive row of beer taps and twenty empty tables. For the most part the place had that rustic patina common in that part of the world but what stood out as exceptional was the huge copper-malting kettle in the middle of the room.

'A bloody brewery! A micro-brewery!' I exclaimed which seemed to delight Giandomenico who had fair English. I looked more closely at the row of taps.

'How many?' I asked.

'Five', came the proud reply with a sweeping gesture of the hand offering them for selection. I laughed and pointed to the end tap. Large cold beers were poured and the four of us pulled up around a small square table. Marcello brought plates of cured beef and local cheese and introductions and explanations were made. The three Italians got to the serious business of village gossip interspersed with Giandomenico's potted history of beer making in the region, how he got started and what he hoped he could do. I made notes in my journal then sat and listened to the others talk, sometimes with my eyes closed, mostly just listening and watching the speakers; mostly just letting the rhythm of the speech and the vibration of the round vowels massage away my tiredness.

Somewhere between the pilsener and the spelt beer, Roberto excused himself and went home leaving me with his phone number and strict instructions to call so that he could pick me up when I was ready. Somewhere after the spelt beer but before the 5.2 per cent alcohol Münchener, Marcello prepared a simple meal of pasta with a sauce made from the local cheese and a little salad. Sometime after the Weizen beer, Marcello brought out a bottle of grappa and I knew it was time to go. Giandomenico insisted he drive me up the hill, or at least let him call Roberto, but I was not having any part of it and doggedly insisted that I walk. It wasn't far, it was impossible to get lost and it was a beautiful night to be out, I argued. There was a little more insisting and counter-insisting needed until we had all filled our insisting quota for the evening and I said my farewell and headed up the hill and into the twisted streets for the 10-minute walk home.

An hour later I was still walking. Keeping direction was easy enough, just walk uphill, but every street I found either didn't go in the right direction or did, but just ended in a dead end after a few hundred metres. There were lots of ways to solve this problem including backtracking to the bar and starting over or going to the top of the village and working down in zigzag pattern, but I was way past, at least two beers past, anything like that. I was just about to select a suitable doorway to sleep in, glad that it was a warm summer's night, when I came to an intersection I remembered from my arrival that afternoon. I jogged up the last 50 metres of lane, gave Just Sue an affectionate slap on the rump as I passed and let myself into the apartment. I was just considering a cup of tea before turning in when I remembered the beer I had put in the freezer that afternoon. I cursed thinking it certainly would have frozen and burst by then but a quick rummage among the ice bricks turned up one Italian lager in icy good health.

Maybe a nightcap, I thought, and wandered out onto the balcony to enjoy the last gasp of a beautiful day. The air seemed to have cleared a little with the evening coolness and, over the roofs of Gordona, I could see the lights of villages scattered down the valley. I opened the beer and caught the rush of frozen foam in my mouth then settled to read the notes I had taken while talking to Giandomenico. It was a good yarn for it seems that beer-making had a long and interesting history in this part of the country. Birrificio Spluga had established a brewery near Chiavenna in 1820 and had continued to operate there until 1957. Giandomenico purchased the name in 2001 in the hope of reviving the beer making tradition in the mountains. Beer, so I discovered, had been a luxury product, expensive to make and to buy. Wine, in comparison, was cheap as everyone made their own. What brought Birrificio Spluga to Chiavenna was the need for special fermentation conditions for the brewing of modern lager beer. Cold and time are the two critical ingredients for good beer fermentation and before commercial refrigeration, Chiavenna was able to offer these in abundance.

The limestone mountains at the head of the Valtelline Valley are riddled with deep caves called crotti, or grottos, which keep a constant temperature between 6° and 8°C and it was these that made the place attractive for beer production. It was only after the introduction of temperature-controlled refrigerated brewery systems in the 1950s that the use of the crotti became uneconomical. But the crotti were not only used for beer making. They were an ancient and central part of life in the valley and were used for the storage and preservation of all manner of local produce through the long and bitter winters. Each family had access to an amount of crotto space allocated by the mayor who applied complicated time-share rules developed over centuries. It was here that the wine, meat, cheese and vegetables to sustain them over the winter were stored.

Over the centuries the crotti became a central part of life in the district. It was, according to Marcello, the job of the old men to go to the crotti each day and bring back the wine and cheese for the day's consumption. This was usually done in the afternoon and the elderly gentlemen would gather in the entrance to their crotti to share their stories and a little of their wine and cheese. Many of the entrances had awnings added for this purpose and some around the town itself eventually developed restaurants under these awnings. These were places that served the traditional dishes of the district, local wine, cheese, brisaola (air-cured beef) and the staple, polenta. Both Giandomenico and his father Marcello were passionate about the culture of the crotti and saddened by its loss to the culture of the refrigerator and the supermarket. When I showed a genuine interest in the story then produced my journal and started to take notes, their faces lit up and the stories flowed and it was this that kept the beer flowing as well.

The clincher for the story, and the reason for my late-night enthusiasm, arrived hot on the heals of our first shot of grappa despite Marcello's disappointment that I had downed it without flinching. It was a simple party trick taught to me years before by some Finns who had a great love of icy cold and fiery vodka and it has stood me in good stead wherever proud men gather with bottles of spirits. The trick is to surreptitiously inhale fully before downing the firewater in a single gulp. Then—and this is the important part—slowly, ever so slowly, exhale through your mouth to clear as much of the fumes as possible. When you have fully exhaled, close your mouth and slowly inhale through your nose. If needed, repeat the process. This simple technique has saved the day with tequila-packing Mexicans, vodka-toting Russians, cunning Thais with Mekong whisky underslung and even a few Aussies who think getting you to choke on the 50 per cent OP rotgut rum they make in the north is a good laugh. Giandomenico hid his disappointment with my spiritual enlightenment (so to speak) and informed me that the local community wanted to keep the tradition of the crotti alive and ran an annual festival of the grottos, the Sagra dei Crotti.

'When is that?' I asked.

'Tomorrow', came the answer.

By the time Maria came in with fresh bread rolls for breakfast, I was up and dressed and full of enthusiasm despite my boozy evening. When I confirmed that there really was a Sagra dei Crotti and that it certainly did start that day, I announced that I would stay over a few days and attend. This obviously pleased her very much. A broad smile spread over her face and she started talking animatedly saying, I suspect, I would have a wonderful time. It was becoming obvious that these people, living on the skirt of the Alps, were immensely proud of their culture and delighted that I was interested. Team Elephant had seen this many times before. Once you are off the tourist trail, people respond beautifully if you show a genuine interest in them and their culture. We are all proud of who we are.

A little after Maria departed, the broad grin of Roberto appeared around the door. The word was out that I was off to the festival. Roberto, speaking fluent moto, opined that it would be silly to take Just Sue as parking would be a problem for a big-hipped girl like her. I should take his moto-scooter instead.

I could park that anywhere and, if I had too much to drink, it knew all the back ways home, or something like that. There was no arguing with the logic or with the generosity so I agreed and Roberto wheeled out the little Vespa. My new nonna was sitting on her chair in the place she had been the previous afternoon ready to exchange a hearty *buongiorno* and watch me mount up and buzz off down through the village. The little scooter was easy to ride after a fully loaded Just Sue and I had a great time zipping along through the traffic. And Roberto was right, I could and did park it anywhere!

First stop was back to the tourist office. The young woman who had served me the day before was on duty and concerned that I had returned to complain about the B&B. But the news that I wanted to attend the Sagra dei Crotti got an improved response and a colour brochure in Italian.

'Do you have anything in English?' I asked.

'No, we don't get asked much.'

There were others waiting for service at the counter so I didn't bother to seek a translation beyond confirming the time for the events in which I was interested (those involving food and wine) and the location of the ticket booth. Confident I had a couple of hours spare, I set off to see the town. Chiavenna was home to about 8,000 souls and straddled the upper reaches of the Mera River with parts of the small old city on either side. The central squares were all being well used for the annual festival with craft markets and displays by the local schools. This part of it looked and felt like local cultural festivals all over the world, which was, in a strange way, comforting. There were plenty of attractive streets in the old city, sweetly restored but not yet a tourist theme park. Down a side street I happened on a hairdresser open for business, checked my own hair length using the accurate 'finger gauge' method and then let myself into the air-conditioned salon for a cut. With these administrative things I have learned to take an opportunity when it presents. Besides, the difference between a good haircut decision and a bad one is, in my case, only two weeks!

Nicely coiffed, or perhaps shorn, I found a cool bar and ordered coffee. The barman spoke a little English. When I told him I was there for the Sagra dei Crotti but couldn't read the brochure he asked to see it, then spent a solid 20 minutes explaining each section while I made notes. By 11:30am, I was in the main square lined up at the ticket booth with enough information to ensure I got the right tickets for my 28 Euro investment. I had selected the four crotti option based within the town precinct. Another option used a shuttle bus for crotti in the surrounding district, which I discounted after having proven myself incompetent at navigating these towns after dark. The first stop, Crotti Crimea, was a 10-minute walk south from the centre of town (although most of the town is a 10-minute walk from the centre) and attached to the Hotel Crimera. I was travelling intentionally light with only a merino sweater in hand and lined up to hand in my ticket and make my way into the cool of the awning erected for the event. First *degustazione* was brisaola and the local Valtellina wine.

Brisaola is air-dried salted beef and is a speciality of the Valtelline. It is usually made from a lean cut like rump or round, which is thoroughly defatted then rubbed with salt and spices: juniper berries, cinnamon or nutmeg are commonly used. The beef is then air-dried for three months until it has lost about half of its weight. It is then sliced wafer thin. The brisaola was surprisingly tender (I was expecting a similar hardness to prosciutto) and sweet. There were brisaola from a number of producers each subtly different in ways I didn't understand. It was, however, all good!

The wine was also Valtellina, a nobbiolo from the village of Vagella. I was vaguely familiar with the nobbiolo grape used in wines from California and Victoria but this version (perhaps a more original cultivator) was more tannic than I had expected. It was certainly an excellent accompaniment to the strongly flavoured brisaola and the long tannin finish was just the thing for a boy brought up on big New World shiraz. I had missed lunch and breakfast had been a bread roll and coffee, so the single glass of vino and a small plate of brisaola was a blessing in disguise. If I could have eaten and drunk more I would have done so and that may have deprived me of a little pleasure at the next stops.

Crotto Osvaldo was a short walk north and was attached to villa of the same name. It had a permanent eatery over the crotto entrance. This was the polenta course and a chance to put away something a little more substantial. The polenta was served soft with tarragon and local sausages and was, as they say, both tasty and nutritious! The highlight, however, was a second but distinctly superior Valtellina nobbiolo. This one had eight summers to soften the tannins and my only regret was that the ration was one glass per head and no go-rounds. By this stage of the evening I had managed a little conversation with one of my eating companions who spoke a little English but his attention was rightly directed to his own party. This didn't bother me at all. I'm an inveterate people-watcher and I was more than content to enjoy the night without the chatter.

Crotto di Preverelli was in the northern end of the town and with the selection of local cheeses and a third glass of wine I was starting to feel very content indeed. The cheeses were all worthy and the wine an altogether lighter red, more of a pinot style but by this stage of the evening I lacked the determination to find out. The last walk was the longest and brought us to Crotto Stampa not far from our start. Here there was more cheese but mainly many and various dessert cakes and a dessert wine, which seemed to be a Sauterne of sorts. I also threw down two shots of espresso before nodding farewell to my travelling companions and starting a search trying to remember what Roberto's scooter looked like. Pick the obvious error here!

The next day I lay low, cooked myself some simple food and caught up on some correspondence. In the evening I went down and had a long chat with Nonna. She asked me in Italian, and in considerable detail, how I had enjoyed the Sagra dei Crotti. I sat side-saddle on Just Sue and gave her a long description of the whole event in English including my opinion on the food and wine. She listened intently, nodding often, interjecting occasionally but mainly saying *si* at the appropriate junctures. When I was finished she imparted a number of the village's very secret secrets and I listened seriously and nodded wisely from time to time. After that I wished her *buona sera* and went back to my balcony to consider the day. Some might think it strange to have a long conversation in two languages and expect much to come of it, but another wise Nonna a long time ago taught me that sometimes just listening is the best you can do.

The next morning Roberto came to see me before I left. We exchanged pleasantries in moto then he wished me a safe journey and a swift reunion with Jo, gave me a strong brotherly hug and presented me with a T-shirt from his Moto Guzzi club. I took it with all of the formality I could muster under the circumstances and made sure he saw me fold it respectfully and pack the ensign in my side bag. Then I fired up Just Sue, gave Nonna a final wave and rode north towards the mountains.

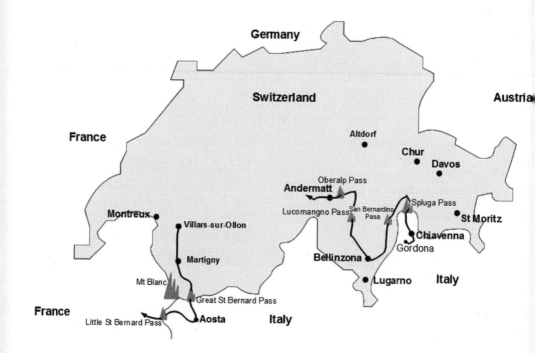

10

SOME OTHER ITALIANS

It was Sunday morning when I rode north through the town of Chiavenna and the congregations were gathered in front of a couple of churches waiting for the nine o'clock mass and catching up on the gossip. Apart from a little churchgoing (and not too much of that) the town looked like a place that had been at a party the night before which, of course, it had. The light traffic made it an easy ride up through a few small villages towards the Passo dello Spluga, which would become the Splügenpass as I slipped over into Switzerland. This gave me some relaxed time to start to put the warmth of my Chiavennan experience into perspective and to be reminded of the true nature of Italy, a country defined by its regions.

This area was first settled by Celts and its main city, now Milan, was important in pre-Roman times. Milan eventually became the capital of the Western Roman Empire and remained important because of its control of the fertile flat lands around Lake Como and the passes over the Alps. Roman control was ceded to waves of Huns including Visigoths, Ostrogoths and eventually, in 569AD, to the Lombards who gave the region its name of Lombardy. Interestingly, the Lombards were duly ousted by the Franks led by Charlemagne but the name endured when Charlemagne declared himself King of the Lombards for reasons that are not entirely clear (to me anyway).

If the early history of the district is confused, things didn't improve during the Middle Ages. Milan was an important city and its control continually shifted as powerful families and nascent states battled for control. In the early 15th century, Milan was declared a republic. In the 16th century it fell under Spanish control through the Iberian arm of the Hapsburg family. By the 18th century the Spanish Hapsburgs had run out of male heirs and control passed to the Austrian Hapsburgs, who incorporated it into the Holy Roman Empire. It was not until the Napoleonic French swept across the Alps from the west in the last gasp of the 18th century that Austrian rule was ended. Napoleon created Milan as the capital of the Cisalpine Republic but French rule was short-lived. The character of political organisation in Europe had changed and the age of the empires had begun. At the post-Napoleon carve-up that was the Congress of Vienna, Lombardy was returned to Austria.

The Milanese revolted against Austrian rule to no good effect, but by the middle of the 19th century the Risorgimento was underway and Italian nationalists were calling for change. Seizing the opportunity the King of Sardinia joined forces with the French to defeat the Austrians and incorporate Lombardy into the Kingdom of Sardinia which, eventually, became the Kingdom of Italy as the modern nation state was created. Sardinia already controlled the lands to the west of Lombardy so this wasn't as big of a stretch, as it may seem.

There were two points that struck me from my quick review of Lombardy history that had filled an idle afternoon in Chiavenna. The first was that the people of this region are an extraordinarily hybrid lot. Wave after wave of invaders took up residence in this strategically important area, each group bringing new vigour to the mix. Only a fascist or a rabid nationalist would dare claim any sort of Italian ethnic purity. This realisation put Mussolini's nation building excesses in perspective. Without a common ethnicity, it would take more than a few monuments to make these people feel Italian. Of course, an Italian Lombardy did emerge, but out of shared enterprise and common purpose not out of slogans and monuments.

Lombardy retains a proud regional identity that draws on its history and the unique geography of the area. It is a culture that lives strong in the valley around Chiavenna. Despite my warmth for the place, the Valtellina had been written off in one of the most prestigious travel guides as one of Italy's less attractive Alpine regions, good only for a little walking and some acceptable skiing. This may explain why Team Elephant doesn't bother with travel guides.

The second blinding flash was simply that the Alps were almost useless as a defence against invasion. While the mountains may look impenetrable, it was clear that any leader with a little determination could and did get through, bringing his army with him. There was, it seemed, no salvation to be found through hiding behind the mountains.

The Splügen Pass is one of the oldest passes through the Alps. It links the Swiss Hinterrhein (Back Rhine) with Chiavenna and a clear run south to Lake Como and the Italian Peninsula, but it has lost its commercial importance since the opening of the San Bernardino Tunnel. The road was given a romantic once-over by Mary Shelley who travelled that way in 1840 and found it exposed, difficult and dangerous. Although the Pass road has certainly been improved since the intrepid Mrs Shelley's day, it is still a dangerous and difficult road, jam-packed with impossible switchbacks, damp one-lane tunnels and sections of broken road surface. Even in its commercial heyday, only light trucks of perhaps 10 tonne capacity would have been able to use it and then only with great difficulty. Life as a transport driver would have been risky and the cost of moving goods exorbitant.

On roads like the Splügen, it is easy to see how isolated the valleys would have been through most of their history. As if to emphasise the limitations, I looked for a stop for a photograph, but the road was so narrow there were few opportunities. When I did find a place, the steep valley sides hindered the view. It was frustrating that the Valtelline Valley was almost directly below me but always just out of sight. An occasional glimpse over my shoulder caught a spectacular vista but a stop, even on a motorcycle, was dangerous. I finally found somewhere to pull over at the tiny village of Montespluga, just inside the Italian frontier. The place was no doubt well situated for the pass economy, but even there I was deprived of a dramatic view back into Italy.

The only people about on a quiet Sunday morning in
Montespluga were a few hardy churchgoers. Even the town dogs
were sleeping in. So I pressed on north and down into Switzerland
urged on now by a desperate need for a mid-morning coffee.
On the Swiss side, I found an equally slumberous village near
enough to the E43 motorway to turn up an open bar with a
place to park Just Sue outside. I stripped off my helmet as I
walked through the door and dumped it unceremoniously on
a table, then got the internationally recognised sign from the
crone behind the bar and stomped through to the rear to find a
toilet every bit as rank as I had anticipated. As I walked back
through to the bar I took note of the place. Three ancient crusty
souls were planted on stools, their tap root legs intertwined with
a regular perch and no doubt drawing sustenance from ample
humus built up over an age. Each had before him a slim larger
glass with the first ice-cold beer of the day placed directly in
front, its thin white cap a perfect creamy centimetre and its
undisturbed condensation evidence that the right moment for
the first sip had not yet come.

I said hello and four wizened heads acknowledged me with
an almost imperceptible movement. I ordered coffee. The crone
raised an eyebrow and turned without enthusiasm towards the
coffee machine. Three heads turned back to study their beers
without further acknowledgement. I looked more closely at the
machine and noted it wasn't well used and changed my order
to a beer. The crone turned back to the beer tap with a nod
to my common sense. The other heads turned and smiled then,
as though the clock had just struck the hour, picked up their
glasses and took a first long satisfying pull. I took my own beer
and settled in a corner at the front where I could watch Just

Sue then pressed the icy wet glass against my forehead and let the condensation run down into my eyes. I lowered the glass under my nose and inhaled its hoppy fume, raised the glass, took a long draw and swallowed slowly. When I opened my eyes, four faces were watching me intently. They gave a slight nod of approval and turned back to their conversation assured that whatever 'other' I was, it was, at the least, a civilised other.

By the time I had drawn off the dregs of my beer a few more customers had arrived. Rusted-on regulars by the look of it, some dressed in church-rig, most turned out for a more crumpled Sunday. Regular places were taken on stools and at tables, others were acknowledged with a nod or a word and regular drinks appeared from behind the bar carried on two of the scrawniest legs I had seen. The newcomers played out the first drink ritual, as was their custom. I thanked the crone, left the change on the counter then went out to climb up on Just Sue, and took a long look up and down a drab and deserted street. Once the motor was fired I gave Just Sue an affectionate slap on the tank. 'Not our idea of a great Sunday, eh girl. Let's go look for some mountains.'

It didn't take much looking. Half an hour of unwinding the contortions of the old road as it twisted under and over the motorway and we were climbing into the mountains again. A few kilometres later, at the place where the E43 disappeared into a tunnel, the old road rose sharply and started to climb towards one of the most commercially important alpine passes. The San Bernardino was just up ahead. The San Bernardino links the Upper Rhine Valley with the Swiss cities of Bellinzona and Lugano and beyond that, the north of Italy. It has been in use since the 15th century, which makes it middle aged in every sense and is often confused by visitors (and at least one guide book of our acquaintance) with the Great St Bernard Pass and the Little St Bernard Pass, both of which are some way off to the west.

The San Bernardino road tunnel was opened in 1967 and takes commercial traffic on a 6.6km shortcut under the mountains— well, mostly under the mountains. If you take the old pass road you get a view of a huge enclosed bridge that is part of the tunnel system. Many motorists would be surprised to find that some part of their tunnel journey had been 100m above the valley floor. As for the old road, it was a mixture of demanding tight bends and fast open sweepers through a pass with a small café, a sad little lake and a cluster of Sunday tourists stopped for lunch. I still had plenty of mountain cheese and sausage so avoided the café crowd and used my little camping stove to boil water for tea while watching the antics of the young parents supervising toddlers by the water.

If there was a downside to the pass it was that the approach from both the north and south was sufficiently uninspiring that I opted to use the motorway for part of the trip rather than battle the weekend traffic. I rated it as a good but not great pass for bike riders and noted that John Hermann assessed it as 'a motorcyclist's delight' but gave it no stars out of a maximum of three in his rating system. Later, while sitting around London watching cable television, I happened on an old episode of the British TV car show *Top Gear* which claimed, much to my surprise, that the San Bernardino Pass road was the best driving road in the world! I realised that the competitions on this show are just a little fun and not meant to be taken seriously, but the San Bernardino wasn't even the best pass I rode that day.

By the time I got down to Bellinzona it was mid-afternoon and hot. I rode straight into the centre of a handy-sized town of about 15,000 souls with everything all but closed for the Sabbath. I was hoping to find a cycling shop open to replace a pair of lost sunglasses. The type I prefer for the motorcycle fit under the helmet well and seal the wind and grit out of the eyes better than other types. After some searching I found a cycle shop with an open door and after more searching I found the proprietor. After an even longer search this time of drawers and cupboards, I found a pair of dark glasses that would do. The first thing I noticed as the owner, his wife and another man (who I think was a visiting friend) made the search, was that they were speaking Italian to each other but addressing me in German. I had finally crossed into Switzerland's southern-most canton of Ticino, annexed from Lombardy and Piedmont in the 15th century by the surrounding Swiss cantons.

In this canton, the overwhelming majority speak Italian and the canton constitution requires, along with the usual freedoms and human dignity, that the canton's Italian history and culture are interpreted within the Helvetic Confederation. When I discovered that this was the Italian part of Switzerland, I thought I might try my luck for the coffee I had missed. I was in luck. While the churches were now deserted after the morning rush, the bars were doing a brisk trade along the main street. The one I picked had other bikes parked outside and a dozen busy tables spilling up and down the pavement. The barista was hard at work behind a huge coffee machine with the aroma of the grind rolling out onto the street in oily waves. This was enough to send morale soaring. The discovery of a bay of quality gelati, however, was the highlight of the day. With a double scoop, a double shot and a shady outside table I settled to enjoy a well-earned break and make a quiet homily to the Italians.

In the Alps, we were constantly surprised by the differences that even a short journey might highlight. Those differences were a reminder of the way communications were limited between valleys separated by only a few kilometres and some high mountains. Each valley developed its own customs including a code of dress for both men and women. The influences on each valley reflected the ease of communication with the outside world rather than the proximity to neighbours. The small differences had persisted into the modern era and had survived the development of road tunnels and the internet. Not that I think good coffee is a small difference!

There were, however, some features of the Alps that were surprisingly consistent from Slovenia to France and this wandering Sunday highlighted one of significance. The rural areas across the Alps were predominately Catholic. I was surprised by this at first because, although swaths of Europe are predominately Catholic, I expected that the Alpine temperament might have tended towards the Protestant ideas of Luther and Calvin. This is particularly so since Calvin's home city of Geneva had a history of busy publishing houses propagating radical Protestant texts. The mountains were also an ideal place for radicals and outlaws to hide from persecution. The French Huguenots and some Italian Protestants were among those who sought such security as the mountains could provide.

While there were exceptions, the city cantons were mainly Protestant while the rural cantons for the most part remained loyal to Rome. Protestantism did make significant inroads into the Alps prompting a long period of instability, which proved a significant issue for the Swiss Federation. While the Swiss are quick to point out that they avoided war for more than 300 years, this claim refers only to war with other states. The cantons remained in a state of constant conflict, most of which originated from this religious divide. Well into modern times, the Catholic/Protestant divide remained a feature of Swiss life. When Mark Twain travelled there in the mid-19th century, he couldn't help but remark on the situation and gently poke fun at the belligerents. In *A Tramp Abroad*, Twain uses his fictional travelling companion Harris, whom he describes as a 'rabid Protestant', to show the absurdity of the sectarian rivalry of the time.

As they travel, Harris continually finds fault with the Catholic cantons and compares them unfavourably with the Protestant. 'In the Protestant cantons you never see such poverty and dirt and squalor as you do in this Catholic one', he says, and then goes on to make more and more outrageous claims. 'It ain't muddy in a Protestant canton when it rains', Harris opines in all mock seriousness, and then assures the reader that 'you never see a goat shedding tears in a Protestant canton.' The exchange reaches its satirical climax when Harris complains that the glaciers in Catholic cantons are dirty, prodding Twain into this exchange:

'What is the matter with this one?'

'Matter? Why, it ain't in any kind of condition. They never take care of a glacier here. The moraine has been spilling gravel around it, and got it all dirty.'

'Why, man, THEY can't help that.'

'THEY? You're right. That is, they WON'T. They could if they wanted to. You never see a spec of dirt on a Protestant glacier. Look at the Rhône Glacier ... if this was a Protestant glacier you wouldn't see it like this ... '.[20]

Twain, like a sensible fellow, gives up on Harris and leaves him to his bigotry and the reader of the time to chuckle at a familiar absurdity.

A few hundred years before Twain made his observations the religious divide was not a joking matter. The appearance in 1560 of the English language Geneva Bible was significant not only for the Alps, but for Protestants across Europe. The Geneva Bible preceded the King James version by a half century and was the first to be mechanically printed and widely available to ordinary people. It also had maps, an index, woodcut illustrations and study notes for each section. The Geneva Bible was used by Shakespeare, Cromwell, Milton and Donne and was taken to the New World by the Mayflower pilgrims. For the 16th-century Catholic Church it was the eye of a perfect storm and a counter-reformation was soon underway.

The counter-reformation was led by the Jesuits, which had been established in 1530 by the crippled ex-soldier Ignatius Loyola specifically for missionary work. The menagerie of princeling rulers governing the Alps were deeply unsettled by the Reformation as their legitimacy, often expressed as a divine right, depended directly on recognition by the Church and often on the direct authority of the Pope. As a result, ample money was found for the Jesuits' campaign, which focused on grass-roots community work. Apart from the usual wars, torture and executions that marked out the counter-reformation, the Jesuits provided a colourful and attractive alternative to the rather dour message of the Protestants. This struck a chord in the mountains where churches were lavishly redecorated and passion plays provided a form of mass entertainment. The famous play at Oberammergau is a vestige of this Jesuit initiative. Although the religious wars continued into the 18th century, by the end of the 17th century the new doctrine of Protestantism had profoundly changed Europe. In the rural Alpine regions, however, the Jesuits had prevailed and it remains a land of ornate Baroque churches, passion plays and a statue of Christ-crucified outside the village.

Victualled and refuelled, I pushed Just Sue off to the north-west, over the Passo del Lucomangno and back to the Rhône Valley and Central Switzerland. The exploration of the Italian Alps, however, was far from over. A few weeks later, Jo had been reunited with the team and we were rested after our stay in Villars-sur-Ollon. With cold wet weather predicted, we rode south through the Swiss town of Martigny heading for the Great St Bernard Pass, the Italian city of Aosta and the last Italian enclave in the Western Alps.

There are records of the Great St Bernard Pass from 400BC and it is one of six passes that are considered possible routes used by Hannibal in 218BC. It is probably the oldest pass in the western Alps. Both Aosta and Martigny have extensive Roman ruins from a time when they guarded the southern and northern access to the pass. There have been many new roads and adjustments made over the centuries but a section of the old Roman road is still visible and usable near the top of the pass at an altitude of 2,469m.

The road up to the pass has been remade many times and we found it crowded with a steady flow of commercial and tourist traffic up to the place where the old road veers off to the pass and the new road takes the burden of heavy transports and disappears into a tunnel. From there on up neither the road nor the scenery were interesting enough for the usual touristy stops and back-tracks. I stopped Just Sue in the pass on a steep section of road where I thought we would be able to see her from any of the cafés plying trade for the bussed-in visitors.

The Great St Bernard Pass is famous for its monastery, established in 1049AD by Bernard, Archdeacon of Aosta, and for the St Bernard dogs used by the monks to sniff out travellers buried in the snow. The story goes that some of the dogs were equipped with a barrel of beer (not brandy) to revive the rescued, but this is another of those alpine legends that may not be entirely true. One version I heard was that a barrel was fixed to the collar of a dog as a stunt for a visiting journalist in the 1830s and the story just got out of hand from there. Even if this version is apocryphal, it is such a good yarn that I don't hesitate to record it here! The monastery was well equipped to cater for the travelling public of the day, which commonly included pilgrims to Rome from the holy city of Canterbury in England. There was a range of services available in addition to food and shelter and the monastery even ran its own morgue so that those searching for missing relatives might have a place to start.

Lest you feel I am being harsh with one of the great passes, I am not the first to find the journey less than stimulating. In his 1862 guidebook to Switzerland, John Murray made the following judgement:

'This pass is more remarkable in an historic and romantic point of view - on account of its   Hospice, monks, and dogs— than for its scenery, which is inferior to that on most of the other great passes.'[21]

Two of the monastery buildings are still in the Pass, although both date from the Middle Ages, and there are some dogs kept there in the summer for the tourists. These days, the important work of the monastery, and the dogs, is fleecing the tourists who use the old roads in large numbers every summer. But, it was always so. With the 19th-century tourist invasion of the Alps, the monks grew rich providing services to the travelling public. When Dickens passed this way, he found the monks 'are a lazy set of fellows ... rich and driving a good trade in in-keeping'[22] Other less distinguished travellers made similar or more severe comments. Nonetheless, many owed their lives to the shelter of the hospice. Murray noted that '300 may be sheltered; and between 500 and 600 have received assistance in one day.'[23]

Napoleon came through the Pass in 1800 with an army on his way to war with Austria and the chance to do away with our friend Andreas Hofer. He, however, didn't pay his hospice bill of 40,000 francs, an account that remained outstanding until settled with a token payment by French President Mitterrand in 1984. It is this pass that is recorded in the heroic painting of Napoleon crossing the Alps on his prancing white stallion painted in 1801 by Jacques-Louis David and the tourist shops had a range of reproductions for sale including one particularly tasteful version printed on a beer stein. We resisted the temptation to pack one in the saddle-bags. Anyway, as we had noted back in Villars, General Bonaparte made the crossing mounted on a sure-footed mule.

At least we are sure that Napoleon did cross the Great St Bernard. It is not so clear that his predecessor Hannibal did so. I was surprised to find dozens of references, of varying degrees of scholarly authority, debating Hannibal's true crossing point.

There are several websites that still debate the options. The most impressive investigation, however, was a two-volume work by John William Law published in 1866 that analysed every reference to the event through more than 600 excruciating pages. His conclusion, like all the others, is inconclusive. The problem is simple enough. The record of the event comes to us primarily from the Roman historians Polybius and Livy who wrote well after the Punic Wars and could not have based their record on an eyewitness accounts. Roman hearsay, it seems, is no more accurate than any other.

We didn't linger in the Pass. The museum and the monastery were of little interest and we had walked, jogged, ridden and driven on Roman roads before so didn't join the conga line of bus tourists, which snaked up to a short section of cobbled antiquity. We also didn't bother with a coffee. Everywhere was crowded and as the long lunch was then underway, we knew the wait would not be worth the reward. Besides, the day was unseasonably hot even at over 2,000m, so an early stop in the city of Aosta seemed like a good idea.

The ride down was pleasant enough despite the heavy traffic but in the last desperate flush of hot weather for the year, we were sweltering by the time we turned off the bypass road to find the centre and a faded hotel with lock-up security for Just Sue. With an early stop, there was plenty of time to see the town's more interesting sights. Aosta was established by the Roman Emperor Augustus to protect the southern approach to the Pass. The settlement was called Augusta Praetoria Salassorum, which was eventually contracted to Aosta, and we found a busy struggle-town complete with Roman ruins and some usefully wide streets. The walls of the old city were remarkably intact.

Often, old town walls are demolished for new development or plundered for stone, so Aostans are lucky to have their little piece of history still recognisable. The original grid pattern of a Roman town is also easy to see within the walls. This being Italy, we found a pizza joint with a good view of the old gates and washed down the house special with several ice-cold Italian lagers.

Aosta has the honour of guarding two St Bernard passes. The Great St Bernard that we had crossed that day from Switzerland and the Little St Bernard Pass that would take us on to France. Not that St Bernard's name would have been of interest to the Romans who were long gone by the time Bernard of Menthon established a hospice for travellers in the 11th century. Aosta also gives its name to the region of Valle d'Aosta. Bordered by France in the West, Switzerland in the north and, the much larger and better known, Piedmont in the south, Valle d'Aosta is the smallest of the Italian regions and the only one with a single province. Like the other valleys of the far north of Italy, it retained a recognisable regional identity and managed to keep a good level of autonomy during the long period of the Middle Ages. This may have been thanks to being cut off from the outside world for regular periods each year. These days, the region describes itself as 'semi-autonomous'. I am not sure what that means for Italian provincial governance, but French and Italian are both considered official languages.

On the morning we departed we took our computer down to reception to take advantage of a strong WiFi signal for a Skype call. The family who ran the old place were having coffee around the reception desk, no doubt discussing the day ahead. Someone found us the coffee and bread rolls that pass for breakfast in those parts. The family was speaking a language that I didn't recognise at all; a little like French perhaps, but not the French I struggle with. When the rush had cleared I asked about it.

'It's the local dialect; a type of French', answered the son, 'everyone here speaks it.'

'Yes', I said, 'of course they do.'

An hour later we were climbing through the suburbs and weaving around the roadworks on our way to the Little St Bernard Pass. It was lower, less touristy and a place where there would be no wait for a quick shot of coffee. We were followed into the café by two fellows travelling in a small hatchback. They introduced themselves and asked if we were travelling west. We were. Could we return a hotel key in the next town taken by mistake? We could. They offered money and I refused. They offered to buy us coffee. I agreed and asked the barman for a triple shot. Everyone laughed and shook hands.

As well as the café, the Pass also had a large bronze of St Bernard right beside the road. The plinth, which elevated the bronze to 3m, was weathered to a pile rock and concrete in a dramatic testimony to the savagery of the climate. St Bernard was pointing down the road towards Aosta as though he was calling to his followers, 'It's that way you fools, that's where they make the good coffee and ice cream!' I liked the statue a lot and spent a long time trying to get a quality photograph. Then, once the camera was packed and Just Sue primed for the run down the mountain, I called out to the statue.

'Not today Bernard, we're off to France for lunch.'

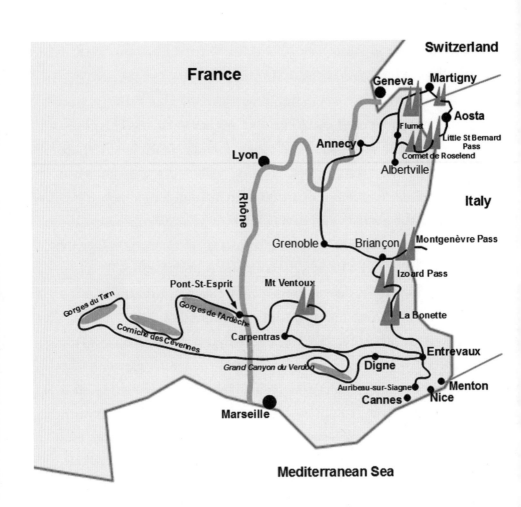

11

THE FRENCH ALPS

And so, Team Elephant finally rolled over another border and dropped into France. We also dropped into cooler weather. It was mid-autumn, the long hot summer was over and the children were back at school. Europe was back at work. We unpacked the cold weather liners for our riding suits and started to take an interest in the weather forecast each evening. As we looped through the French Alps to the west and south of Mount Blanc, the sky started to assume that grey and menacing look more familiarly European than the antipodean azure of those first days in Slovenia.

We are old hands in France and over a number of years riding motorcycles there we have criss-crossed the country from Belgium to the Mediterranean, from Arcachon on the Atlantic to the plains of Champagne. It has remained one of our favourite places; an easy country in which to travel and live well; a place where a couple of ageing desperadoes on a motorcycle are unexceptional and welcome. Like every other part of France, the French Alps had a distinctly French feel. Of course, every alpine country has its own identity, but we had long decided that the overall feel of the Alps was predominately German. This was not just a matter of language as many dialects and languages are spoken. Rather it appeared to us in the very mundane things of life like the food, the neatness of the villages, the ubiquitous chalets and an orderly traffic flow when conditions were poor.

We are not the only ones to notice the French difference. Several commentators have questioned if the French part of the Alps and, in particular, the mountains in the Alpes Maritimes, which sweep down to the sea at the Côte d'Azur, are part of the Alps at all. Even though the mountains are part of the same geological movement, and despite many peaks being of alpine stature, some feel the place just doesn't look alpine. It seemed to us that it would be hard to make that case in the areas contiguous with Switzerland around Mont Blanc, but as you travel south into Provence, the alpine areas become less and less 'the Alps' as most people think of them.

Whatever the argument, some differences were plain on our first night. We had found a small auberge just outside the village of Flumet. It was empty in the short hiatus between the end of the summer holidays and the start of the ski season and we were pleased to have the place to ourselves. We stowed our gear and then propped against the deck rail overlooking the valley to watch the long shadows sweep the last of the day up a slope behind the village and to enjoy a drink with the owners. They had children, a little younger than ours, and assorted moto parked under the balcony so there was enough in common to keep the chat going past the usual dinner hour. When someone noticed the time, our hosts became concerned that we might be hungry. We shrugged. There was no rush and we had nowhere else to be. A long list of food options was rattled off so quickly that in our mellow state we couldn't be bothered to work out what they might be in English. Something simple and light, whatever you are going to have yourselves, was our reply. I was tired and relaxed and would have settled for a toasted sandwich, or maybe another beer and a packet of nuts.

What arrived was an unexceptional family meal, except that it was exceptional. The salad was freshly cut and full of crunch, the local sausages were superior and accompanied by lashings of fresh, perfectly cooked vegetables, a carafe of local pinot was serviceable and brought out the best in a single local cows' cheese and the last of the season's stone fruit made a clean finish to the meal. It was a nice reminder of the simple things we like about France and an easy example of one of the things that make this northern part of the French Alps a little different.

Jo and I are both enthusiasts for good food; not foodies, but folk who like to eat good healthy food that has been well prepared. Eating has been an enjoyable part of our travel adventure over the years but the Alps have never fired our enthusiasm. This is not surprising when the history of the area is considered. The alpine soils (particularly in the limestone areas) are poor, the growing season is short and the range of produce limited by climate. In addition, difficult communications and the general poverty of the alpine economy before the rise of tourism limited the trade in foodstuffs. Early travellers in all areas of the Alps commented on the poor diet and poor health of the locals. Baedeker and Murray produced well-used guides for the Alps in the mid-19th century. Both commented on the prevalence of chronic disease and poverty among the locals. Many other chroniclers agreed and the incidence of cretinism and goitre are commonly mentioned. Both of these conditions resulted from a lack of iodine and point to the limited diet and poor soils of the region.

Artificial fertilisers, a strong economy and better roads have certainly made a dramatic improvement in the range of goods available, but the culinary traditions were well formed before these changes and reflect past limitations in supply and climate. It seems to me, however, the development of a modern mixed-cuisine culture takes more than access to ingredients. It also requires a substantial and integrated migrant community to cause the fusion of new and old styles and ingredients. You only have to look at the development of Vietnamese and Thai food in Sydney, San Francisco or Vancouver, or the new-style Indian and Pakistani cuisine of London to see how this works. The Alps have not had modern mass migrations like these other places. Cheese and cured meats (generally pork but also beef in some areas) were the traditional way of preserving protein for the long winter. Potatoes and other root vegetables survived in the cellars but it wasn't long into the cold weather before the greens were reduced to pickles and preserves with the ubiquitous sauerkraut keeping the scurvy at bay.

As part of the research for this journey I had found some background reading on the cuisines of the Alps. I read it through then placed it on the book shelf with a hundred other cooking books and there it has stayed. None of this is to say that the food on offer across the Alps is inadequate. Like other travellers, we ate cheaply and well and often found the hearty meals comforting after a long day in the saddle. It is simply to point out that if you desire a culinary adventure, then you might be better looking elsewhere.

This part of France, in the shadow of Mount Blanc, has well developed resort towns catering to a year-round trade. The winter ski crowd is replaced seamlessly each spring with walkers, cyclists and paragliders. Each summer brings the climbers, canyoners, bungee jumpers, more cyclists chasing the Tour de France and a family holiday crowd based in Annecy nestled at the top of the lake of the same name. Autumn brings the motorbikes in big numbers and is considered the best time for serious tramping in the mountains. As a result, towns like Annecy are expensive all the time and have a prosperous feel lost from some French provincial towns these days. For us, these are places to buy fuel and enjoy a nice lunch or to do a little sightseeing but they are not generally places to stay. We were, therefore, thankful for the inter-season quiet and the chance for some congenial and cheap digs from which to explore the mountains.

Our base near Flumet was in the middle of a triangle formed by the ritzy ski-towns of Annecy, Albertville and Chamonix. It was ideally placed for a two-day loop back into Switzerland over the Col de la Forclaz and the famous village of Martigny and back via the Pas de Morgins and a loop almost all the way back to Lac Léman (Lake Geneva). Many of the roads in this area have been made famous by the Tour de France. As a result, thousands of ordinary amateur cyclists converge on this part of the Alps each year to test themselves over the same roads they see ridden by the professionals. Apart from the obvious social benefit of so many people doing so much exercise, the cyclists are big business and are well catered for by the French. We had just crossed into France from the Petit St Bernard Pass and started a relaxed ramble over the Cormet de Roselend when we noticed the cyclists' kilometre-markers by the road. Relatively small and placed where a cyclist would easily see them, the markers provided the name of the climb, the distance to the pass or summit (or from the summit on the way down) and the gradient for that kilometre expressed as a percentage. Some also had the overall gradient for the climb.

As we had seen on the high passes in Austria, Italy and Switzerland, the range of cyclists was also impressive. There were the expected groups of young silverbacks keen to test their strength against the mountains, but there were also many older, less fit, riders on bikes of a quality that might be described, tongue in cheek, as pedestrian. They invariably stopped at the pass to savour their small victory and a celebratory cold beer before pulling on a warm jacket and hurtling back down the mountain. To be honest, I felt a little twinge of envy when I saw them on the road. There is a lot of satisfaction in driving those little machines up big hills powered by nothing but your legs and a good supply of bananas and for no reward other than a righteous beer at the top.

Cycling in the Alps is not a new fad. In the year 1900, barely 20 years after the invention of the safety bicycle and less than 20 years after John Dunlop invented the flat tyre, C. L. Freeston published *Cycling in the Alps*. Along with practical advice on preparation, fitness, travel arrangement and so on, the guide describes many of the passes we had crossed on our own Alps journey in hair-raising detail. Considering the unpaved state of many roads and the fact that most bicycles of the time were equipped with a fixed-wheel and had no brakes (other than the muscular legs of the rider), these early cyclists must have been a brave and hardy bunch. More than anything else, however, the existence of this early guidebook is evidence of the democratisation of travel, which took place at the time. The bicycle was, along with the railways, instrumental in moving alpine tourism within reach of an emerging European middle class.

It was a stunning revolution and it happened with breathtaking speed. Within five years of Dunlop's invention, the first modern bicycles with pneumatic tyres were in mass production and the Cyclists' Touring Club had been established. The club eventually grew to more than 60,000 members. The irrepressible Cook was conducting guided bicycle tours of Normandy by 1896 and by the turn of the century, cycle touring in the Alps was commonplace. The bicycle more than any other invention liberated an urban industrial generation by providing personal transportation at a price affordable to those of modest means. When used in conjunction with the railway, it allowed a level of freedom not seen before. The wealthy may not have liked it much, but the common folk were on the move, things were changing in the Alps and business was good. And business remained good, right up to 1914 and the start of the Great War.

Back in France, we were also back in Napoleon country. We had crossed his path in other places on this journey and there was no doubt his influence on the Alps had been significant, if short-lived. Here in France the spectre of Napoleon is still vivid and nowhere more so than the French Alps. Napoleon had a special affection for the people of the Alps. As a Corsican, he would have been born into a culture dominated by mountains with all of the idiosyncrasies that can entail. He certainly knew enough to cross the Great St Bernard Pass on a mule. If he was ever taken by alpine scenery, he made no mention of it, but his wife Joséphine was more obviously impressed. She invited a Swiss farmer and his family (with some mountain cattle) to set up an alpine chalet near Paris. The people of the Alps had always supported Napoleon, but it was his return from exile on the Mediterranean island of Elba in March 1815 that cemented the relationship. Napoleon had been exiled after the defeat of France in 1814 by a coalition of six European states. He was, officially at least, nominated as the sovereign of Elba and was able to keep a personal guard of 600 men. If this seems like a bad idea in hindsight, it should be noted that many thought it so at the time. Napoleon spent about 300 days on the island before making his escape and landing with a small force on the French coast at Golfe-Juan near present-day Antibes and then setting out for Paris and the crazy 100 days that would end at Waterloo. Napoleon's progress north from the Mediterranean was halted near Grenoble by a force loyal to the new king. Undaunted, Napoleon walked forward alone, showed himself to the garrison, declared himself their general and asked if any man would shoot him. Rather than take up the offer, the defenders cried out '*Vive l'Empereur!*' and joined the growing force marching north into history. Napoleon was so impressed with his reception by the Alpine French that he ordered the construction of a number of roads over alpine passes, leaving a more enduring and commercially useful legacy to the locals.

All of this legendary stuff was immortalised in 1935 when the French inaugurated a road from Antibes through Grasse and Digne then on to Grenoble called the Route Napoleon, or the N85 for the less romantic. The route is marked with the

Emperor's flying eagle symbol. It has informative little history boards at strategic stops and is a favourite tourist drive in the south. We rode some of the more interesting sections of the N85 and, apart from a surfeit of snail-like campers, it proved to be a pleasant enough way to get to or from the Côte d'Azur. The better motorcycle roads, however, are off to the east crossing back and forward into Italy and it was these roads we chose for the last leg of our journey.

Napoleon's final incarceration on the remote Atlantic island of St Helena was significant for the Alps in another very practical sense. It marked the end of the Napoleonic Wars and the start of a long period of relative peace. Even the short Franco-Prussian War of 1870–1 did no more than ruin a season and a single staging of the passion play at Oberammergau. It was this peace, the backed-up wealth of a fast industrialising Britain and the freedom derived from trains and bicycles that developed the Alps we find today. Within a few years of Napoleon's final exile, the Cook's Tours' thousands would invade the Alps and Cook himself would be dubbed, the irony no doubt intended, the Napoleon of Excursions.

In general, the watershed of the French Alps runs along the border with Italy and there are a number of useful high passes and lesser roads crossing back and forth across the frontier. These were the roads that were most of interest to us for our intended route south to the Cote d'Azur. To the west, the mountains drop down to the Rhône River Valley with the French Massif Central beyond the river and well away from the Alps. The Massif covers a huge area, more than 500km long and 340km wide, and is in the shape of an inverted triangle with the apex somewhere west of Montpellier and the eastern side running along the Rhône.

We were aware of the Massif Central having ridden across it in several directions in the past but those had always been transit journeys using the better roads. We intended to take the same sort of approach on this journey until a chance reading of a Uniting Kingdom rider's blog caused us to reassess our route.

A little research on the gorge roads in the south of the Massif was enough for us to decide a change of direction. They were considered some of the best riding in France and, with the weather holding and with no shortage of time, there would never be a better time to go. We replanned our route to take us south down the Alps parallel to the Italian border to the vicinity of Entrevaux, then west across the Rhône with a long loop around the bottom of the Massif Central to recross the Rhône and return to our alpine route in the foothills above Grasse. We did enough route planning to cover a few days, then tracked south towards Briançon.

The Briançon, we found a day later, had a number of features typical of ancient alpine towns. The site pre-dates the Romans (who called it Brigantium) and guards access to the Col de Montgenévre. It is also the highest city in the European Union at 1326m altitude. The old city of today rests on a plateau above the confluence of the Durance and Guisane rivers and was built in the 17th century to defend the pass against the Austrians. The newer parts of town scatter out over the valley floor at the foot of the plateau. We arrived in Briançon early in the day with the intention of a little touristic diversion and some lunch before we moved on. I parked Just Sue on a steep slope outside the old city and made a simple mistake. Before I explain the mistake I probably need to say something about how motorcycles work compared with a how a car works for the sake of non-riders.

Motorcycles don't have a parking brake. If you park your bike on a slope, the idea is that you leave it in gear and allow the engine to stop it rolling. In addition, bikes need a side stand to stop them falling over when stopped. A side stand, however, can be a danger if you inadvertently ride off without retracting it. For this reason, modern bikes like Just Sue have a cut-out switch attached to the stand that stops the engine if the bike is in gear when the stand is down. Bikes also have their headlight hard-wired on so that they cannot be turned off. This is supposed to be a safety measure.

So, back to the car park. With a steep slope, I left the bike in first gear, kicked the side stand down which stopped the engine, let out the clutch so the engine would stop the bike rolling and then started to lean forward over the tank to turn off the ignition. That last part is where the problem started. Just as I put down the stand, two German riders, with well-travelled bikes parked nearby, came over for a chat. They were from Hamburg and had seen the Kangaroo stickers on our luggage. We climbed off and introduced ourselves. By the time we had exchanged our stories and said farewell, we had forgotten all about Just Sue. I took the ignition key and we headed off into the old city to find the tourist office and a public toilet. When we returned, we discovered the long period Just Sue had spent sitting with her ignition and lights on long had been enough to fully flatten her ageing battery. The engine would not crank!

This brought on the usual round of self-recrimination and a bad temper from me and grim resignation from Jo. We unpacked all of the luggage from the bike and pushed it to a place where I could get a clear roll down a reasonable hill. I got Just Sue rolling, hoisted myself on board, clicked through to third gear and let out the clutch. The engine failed to fire. A second attempt failed. A third attempt fired the engine with a bang. We repacked, rode around for an hour with the engine running fast, then found a hotel where we could park on a hill and decided to call Briançon home for a night. I am not sure there is a moral in this story beyond the simple point that we have been riding bikes for a lifetime and we still do dumb things that bring us unstuck. Everybody does. The important thing is not to beat yourself up about it. We often chanted to our offspring, don't panic and keep going. There is always a solution out there somewhere if you don't bring yourself undone!

Our ramshackle hotel near the railway station was comfortable enough and fed us well and cheaply. Just Sue fired into life with a gentle roll the next morning and the road south from Briançon over the Col d'Izoard was exhilarating. A little further south, the Parc National du Mercantour held the last high alpine road— not a pass this time but the loop road around the top of the mountain La Bonette. A sign claimed that this was the highest sealed road in Europe but we doubt this is true. The road is also a Tour de France favourite. We dutifully rode up to the highest point taking care for the safety of several hundred British cyclists on an organised ride to raise money for the charity Help for Heroes, and took the necessary photos to mark our arrival at the (claimed) top of the European motoring world. But it was not a great mountain road and we started to realise that, despite the altitude, the high alpine roads were behind us.

South from La Bonette, it took us a few more days to drift down through the Alpes de Provence over a 100km of back roads, narrow gorges and tiny villages to the ancient town of Entrevaux tightly packed beside the River Var with its old defensive works clinging improbably to the steep valley wall above. The original defences had been built across a narrow gorge to repel Saracen invaders in the 11th century and the defensive scheme of the place is still obvious from a vantage point above the town on the northern side of the river. The day we visited, a troop of men dressed as Knights Templar were busying themselves guarding the front gate and parading in front of the old city walls much to the delight of the tourists.

Entrevaux was as far as we would go south for a while so we turned west over almost-deserted rural back roads heading towards the village of Comps-sur-Artuby and access to the Grand Canyon du Verdon. This French version of a Grand Canyon, carved out of the limestone plateau by the River Verdon, is nowhere near as grand as the US version carved out by the Colorado. It is, nonetheless, an impressive hole in the countryside with views that I don't hesitate to call grand. We took the road along the southern bank through the length of the gorge to the point where it enters Lac de Sainte Croix, then followed the northern bank back to the east. The road was narrow and twisting and busy with tourists and bikers. There were enough blind corners shielding bumbling hatchbacks, slowed and wandering, looking for a view of the gorge, to make it a cautious ride in some parts. Despite its popularity, it made for a wonderful day on a motorbike made perfect by a picnic lunch in a park overlooking the lake.

The Verdon is popular for paddling and rafting sports in the summer and, while the numbers were well down by the time we arrived in the autumn cool, the roads and the river were still busy. We took note that most of the camping and cabin accommodation businesses had already closed after the summer season and were left to speculate about how crowded the place would be during the holidays. Our bet is the single gorge road would be bumper to bumper for a couple of months and that late autumn is the time for a biker to make an appearance.

Our plan was to ride west to the Rhône the next day so we set out early across the back roads. The weather had other ideas, however, and we stopped several times to don our rain suits only to haul them off our sweaty bodies a few kilometres further on when the sun appeared. By the time we were rolling though shallow valleys of lavender farms to the east of Mazan I was all for making another plan. It had been four hard months on the road, our time off at Villars already seemed distant and we were both tired. We have always tried to have a few days off each week and to avoid travelling every day, but we had been pushing hard on this journey always aware that the weather could change quickly and drive us out of the mountains for weeks. When Just Sue started to run a little rough under load, we took it as a sign and checked the map. Carpentras was just up ahead and seemed to be a reasonably sized town where we might find a workshop. It would do just fine. Team Elephant needed a holiday.

The rest of the day was busy with our change of plan but we had no trouble finding a compact but comfortable villa for rent about 10km out of Carpentras in the village of Saint Didier. And, by the time we were enjoying the last of the day over a glass of local wine, we had taken the villa for a week, emptied our gear out of Just Sue's side and top boxes, refilled them with groceries at a Carpetras supermarket and discovered the location of a reputable Suzuki dealer. We had a comfortable place to stay with a refrigerator full of food, a respectable wine to drink and we could sleep in for the first time in weeks. Bliss.

A day after we had arrived we had managed to establish our version of domestic nirvana sleeping late, walking, cooking, writing and reading. The Suzuki dealer found and fixed the problem with Just Sue without difficulty. An air intake had not been properly secured when the replacement engine was fitted causing variation in the fuel–air mix under load. I had a few other minor repairs done at the same time and bought a new pair of lightweight gloves to round out the bike maintenance. We visited Carpentras each day to check our emails at a café and did what wandering there was to do around the old city. By the time our week was up we had settled into such a comfortable existence that it was a wrench to load up and move on. Somehow this is always the way with our journeys.

We often come home from an adventure to have our friends ask how the holiday was, as though living on the back of a bike for a few months or a year is like a Mediterranean cruise or a week at the beach. Our response is usually to say that if what we do is a holiday, then we need to get back to work for a rest! Maybe it is a conceit on our part but we have come to think of a journey as a special activity not related to a holiday; something that has its own rewards that need to be earned through application. The stories we hear along the way have as much value for the way they have been discovered as for their content. For us, even the simple things we discover through our own efforts are of worth, while the profound loses its impact when it is handed out with a cut lunch. Shielded by hubris like this, our journeys are guided mainly by our curiosity and willingness to investigate and made worthwhile by what we discover, often about ourselves, along the way.

It was that kind of silly logic that meant we left Carpentras heading for a long sweep back to the east over Mount Ventoux. We had been on our Massif Central detour for more than a week, we still hadn't crossed the Rhône, and we were now heading away from the river. We only had the streaker's excuse: it seemed like a good idea at the time! Mount Ventoux is well known as a regular feature of the Tour de France, where it has earned the nickname the Beast of Provence. It is geologically part of the Alps but stands separate from the other high mountains and towers above the surrounding hills, its bare limestone top devoid of vegetation and open to the fierce winds that give it its name. The roads up to the summit are well made with long stretches of sweeping bends, which invite spirited riding, or driving. These roads have been used for many years by car manufacturers to test the braking systems on cars and it is a place where not-so-secret secret prototypes have been captured on film by the motoring press assisted by a clear view over the barren hillside.

We stopped just short of the summit to capture the view and inspect a monument by the side of the road. A granite stone marks the place where British cyclist Tom Simpson died just short of the summit on the 1967 Tour de France still clipped into his pedals. There is some debate about the cause of death but dehydration exacerbated by amphetamines and alcohol is thought to be the culprit. Cyclists had left a few mementos on the site but it seemed a rather bleak place to us; the sort of place you would stop for a few minutes and then keep moving before the wind chilled you to the bone. There was the usual cluster of celebrating cyclists outside the weather station that dominates the summit and a fine view in all directions but nothing to keep us there exposed to the first of the season's Mistral winds.

Just Sue plunged down the northern side of the mountain

into worsening weather and we let-out for the Rhône, finally crossing and starting the climb to the Massif Central at Pont-Saint-Esprit. We settled for lunch on the edge of the main square and somewhere between finishing our soup, and the arrival of our coffee the threatening rain finally arrived with a crash. We watched Just Sue sit in the rain and ordered more coffee.

'Nice town', said Jo.

'Mmm.' The rain thundered down. 'Think we should stay?'

'Possibly', she said, po-faced.

'Definitely!' I answered with a laugh.

It took more than an hour squelching around in the deluge to find a hotel and get undercover in a decrepit place. Its main virtue was a dry underground garage. We were warm and comfortable again but our detour to the Massif Central had started to feel a little epic. Over food in a hotel room so bare our voices echoed, we decided to take some of our own advice, harden up and get on with it. We decided to ride the three scenic routes we had selected the next day and then turn east again and get back to the Alps in the following day. It was only a few hundred kilometres; how hard could it be?

The three scenic routes we had in mind were Gorges de l'Ardèche, the Corniche des Cévennes and the Gorges du Tarn, and, the next day we had picked up the river Ardèche and were disappearing into the first gorge 30 minutes after we had found our way out of Pont-St-Esprit. By lunch we were just through Gorges de l'Ardèche and by the time the shadows were long enough to have me thinking about a night stop and a cold beer we were still only part-way through the Corniche. The problem wasn't the traffic, of which there was little, nor was it the roads, which were easier and quicker than those we had become used to in the Alps. The problem, if you could call it a problem, was simply that this was such a wonderful place to ride that we slowed our own progress through constant stops for stunning scenery and the exploration of small villages. Why hadn't someone told us about this place before? We had found some of the nicest parts of France and it came as a surprise. There must have been a reason.

We found a neat and prosperous village with a well-preserved historic centre and a quaint family-run hotel with a friendly dog mooching around the bar and decided that the delay was worthwhile. The next day we followed the gorge south-west down the Tarn for another brilliant ride punctuated by lots of photo stops and sidetracks to explore local attractions, then turned north to loop back towards the Alps.

The weather was kind to us for our charge back across the country to resume our Alps mission and, while the ride lacked the drama of our journey west through the gorges, it was pleasant ramble through a part of rural France that was new to us. A week later in a car park near the Côte d'Azur we finally worked out why we hadn't heard about the gorges from the many bikers we had met on our journey. We struck up a conversation with a couple of British riders who were keen to do some of the better roads. Jo started to direct their attention to the gorges on the Massif when I interrupted and insisted that the best roads were to the north and into Switzerland. Later, Jo asked me what 'that' had been about.

'I'm not telling anyone about that place', I insisted.

'You're kidding!'

'I don't want the place full of bikes when we go back.'

She gave me that 'I don't believe you sometimes' look and

made that little sound of exasperation parents perfect.

Our return to the east and to the Alpes Maritimes brought us back to our main interest with only a few kilometres still to ride and we finally dropped into the foothills behind the Côte d'Azur city of Cannes. We found an expensive villa near the village of Auribeau-sur-Siagne to spend a lazy week. Our slow progress through this last section of our journey may have reflected a slight melancholy at having come to the end of our alpine loop. Even though we had logged over 5,000km of riding to cover a mere 800km of distance there still seemed to be dozens, perhaps hundreds, of minor roads that seemed in desperate need of inspection. Every time we studied the maps, we found places we had missed or decided not to visit because we lacked the time or, more likely, the determination. Still, we were there, almost at the end, with only one important stop remaining. The town of Menton, where the Alps meet the sea, was still a short ride further.

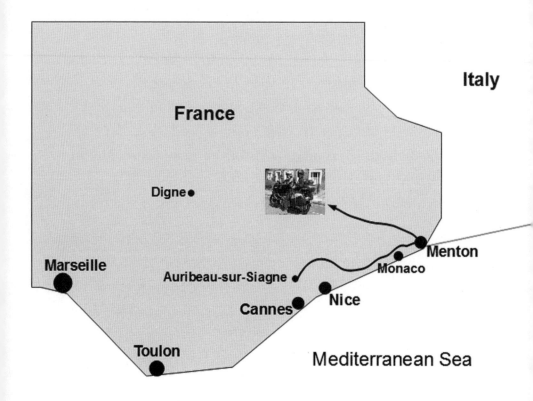

Italy

France

Digne●

Marseille

Auribeau-sur-Siagne●

Cannes

Nice

Monaco

Menton

Toulon

Mediterranean Sea

12

A LONELY GRAVE
BY THE SEA

Our decision to indulge in an upmarket villa instead of our usual budget accommodation wasn't entirely out of character. We had arranged for our daughter, son-in-law and granddaughter to meet us on the Côte d'Azur so they could get a last burst of warmth before the long London winter. It turned out to be an inspired decision. We had a relaxed week of touristy exploration, sea-side lunches and a little swimming in the tepid Mediterranean at one of the famous beaches. For both Jo and I, spending time with our granddaughter has always been a priority. We had made a pact when she was born to be part of her life as she grew. I am sure this is common enough for grandparents and I am sure that others like us are faced with the problem of making that happen when their grandchild lives on the other side of the world.

For us it has meant returning to the United Kingdom and

Europe for months every year, the decision to leave a motorcycle permanently in London, the search for a focus for our European travels and the eventual re-discovery of John Hermann's book. The three years of travel and research that followed had seen our granddaughter grow into an engaging pre-schooler and us develop an abiding love of the Alps. It also gave us a chance to get to know and love our son-in-law whose saintly forbearance of our endless intrusion into their lives is a wonder. Besides, no one who has tried would claim that it's easy work wrangling an active three year old. A day spent doing ordinary stuff with a little girl tends to put the Alps into some kind of perspective. In the end, they are just mountains.

Apart from our role as indulging grandparents, we also used our Côte d'Azur stay to get some important maintenance done on Just Sue. I spent a day searching out a Suzuki dealer in Nice to source some new brake pads and the necessaries for an oil change and service. The Alps were tough on brakes. With the bike heavily loaded and Team Elephant often hustling along we had managed fewer than 10,000km from the last set. I changed over the brake pads in a few moments in the driveway of the villa but there was nowhere to park Just Sue sufficiently level to allow me to change the oil. My solution was to pack the equipment for the job into the back-box and ride a few hundred metres to a section of road with a wide flat parking area, which was littered with rubbish. I got organised quickly and had already dropped the oil into a plastic basin purchased cheaply for the purpose when the Municipal Police arrived in their little blue car demanding to know why I was dumping my waste in their pristine waterway. I resisted the temptation to point out that the stream was so polluted that a little of Just Sue's precious bodily fluid wouldn't make any difference, explained why I was there and then went about decanting the oil into several empty containers I had with me and stowing them in the back box.

While this was going on, two more police cars arrived bringing the total number of officers supervising me to five. Two of them, for some reason I didn't understand, started to lend a hand while the others stood by talking on their mobile phones. By the time I was cleaned up and ready to go the discussions with head office were in animated overdrive so I started the bike, thanked the two officers who had assisted and caught the attention of the guy who seemed to be the most senior. I smiled and indicated that I was done and leaving and that the area was the same rubbish tip it had been when I arrived. He stopped talking and stared at me for a moment, then waved me away with a shrug. As I dawdled up the road I slapped Just Sue on the tank.

'That was a mistake, old girl', I said out loud. Just Sue just purred on as a bike should with a belly full of new oil and some nice new brakes. 'We better not do that again.'

During our break at Auribeau-sur-Siagne we avoided thinking about the last leg of our alpine adventure, which would take us to the place where the Alps finally tumble into the sea near the French–Italian border at Menton on the northern end of the French Riviera. Six months before in London we had thought the Riviera was a bizarre place to end a journey through the Alps. Like many others we were probably convinced by the idea of the mystic purity of high mountains. We had the same romantic idea of the place that had lured millions of others to the mountains over two hundred years. We had seen the Alps as clean, unpolluted, isolated and still retaining a sort of natural purity lost to many other places. The Riviera, on the other hand, we saw as a little tacky and artificial. By the time we settled into our rented villa, we had come to a far less romantic view of the Alps. And, by the time I was providing a diversion for the Municipal Police in Auribeau, we understood that the French Côte d'Azur and the Swiss city of Davos really had more in common than either would admit and that both places exist first in our imagination.

Like the Alps, the Riviera is a place created largely out of the imagination of foreigners. Even the name Riviera was invented by foreigners. From the loss of its importance to Romans travelling to Gaul until the end of the Napoleonic Wars, the Côte d'Azur, that section of coast from Cap Camarat near St Tropez to the Italian border, remained a backwater; desperately poor, remote and bypassed by history. Even at the end of European hostilities, there was simply nothing there to attract the class of Briton with the means to travel. Those wealthy souls were on their way to Italy or Greece to avoid the winter chill and discover their western cultural heritage. If Nice boasted the ruins of a Roman past, then this simply provoked the wonder that they had ever gone there at all. Historian Jim Ring summed it up nicely: 'The civilised world created by the Romans along the artery of the Via Aurelia had all but disappeared. After seventeen hundred years of progress all that was left were a few isolated villages, paupered in all but sunshine.'[24]

Sunshine, however, had value, especially to the English who lived compressed into industrial cities plagued with smog, chronic chest infections and tuberculosis, which, by the late 18th century, was killing one Briton in six. By the early years of the 19th century guest-houses in Nice and Cannes were doing a brisk trade catering to English invalids and to their demands for the luxuries of home. The doctors of the time conjured benefits from climate for a whole range of ailments and promoted the advantages of specific Mediterranean towns for particular cures. Whatever the true benefits, the English came in numbers and brought with them all of the trappings of their own culture. The locals were overwhelmed and by the middle of the century, the city of Cannes was an Anglicised colony.

Not that Cannes and Nice relied entirely for their livelihood on English invalids. Noted Englishmen set up summer houses there and attracted others in the way that celebrity always attracts an entourage. Hucksters, carpetbaggers, gamblers and whores followed and the place developed fast and loose as frontier towns generally do. By the time medical opinion had decided that clean mountain air was a better cure for 'ailments of the breast', the invalids had moved up the coast a few kilometres to Menton where the final descent of the Alps into the Ligurian Sea provided respite from the Mistral winds of autumn and better conditions for the frail.

The rest of the history of the Riviera is well known in the broad; queens and gamblers and abdicated kings, movie star princesses, princes who became kings and some who were just frogs, Rothchilds aplenty, Picasso and Matisse, property speculators who were conmen, conmen who ran the place, and rock stars and movie stars who had more money than sense or just not much sense at all. It has 18 golf courses, 14 ski resorts and 3,000 restaurants. Half the world's super yachts are moored there among thousands of other craft of every shape and size, few of which ever go anywhere much. It wasn't a hard place to understand. There are now places like this all over the world. The Riviera was just the first and these days is no more seedy than many others.

For many living far from this place, what they know of the Riviera is filtered through the story of Grace Kelly, the American actress who became Princess Grace of Monaco. But, like a lot about the Riviera, the fairytale of her marriage in 1956 to Rainier Louis Henri Maxence Bertrand de Grimaldi, more easily tagged Prince Rainier III, has plenty of dark undercurrents. Grace, who was the daughter of a Philadelphian businessman of Irish extraction, came to Monaco in 1954 to make the movie *To Catch a Thief* with Cary Grant. Rainier was the one-time dilettante prince, one-time colonel in De Gaul's Free French Forces and, by then, full-time ruler of the 375 acres of the tiny principality of Monaco.

Contrary to the legend, the pair didn't meet during the making of the movie and Kelly had a low opinion of Rainier by reputation describing him as 'a stuffy fellow'. Rainier didn't think much of anything from the New World and had no shortage of beautiful young women interested in his attention. What changed the game was the intervention of one of Monaco's residents, the shipping magnate Aristotle Socrates Onassis, who was by then the richest and most powerful of Rainier's subjects. Onassis wanted the playboy prince married and saw a wedding between a movie star and a prince as the type of fairytale that might reignite a stagnant economy. Brigitte Bardot, Marilyn Monroe and Grace Kelly were considered and Onassis went so far as putting a proposition to Marilyn. The feisty actress replied that given two days alone, of course he'll want to marry me.

Onassis was in cahoots with the prince's religious advisor, the priest Father Francis Tucker. The pair widened the search to include Natalie Wood, Deborah Kerr and Princess Margaret.

Although I doubt that the newly crowned Queen Elisabeth, Defender of the Faith for the Church of England, would have warmed to having her sister convert to Catholicism. In the end, Tucker, who was an Irish-American, pushed for one of his own and a meeting was arranged between Kelly and Rainier when she returned to the Riviera for the Cannes Film Festival. When the Prince showed some interest in the American, Tucker went off to the United States to investigate her background. He had, however, already shown his preference for Grace by sabotaging several other contenders. The romance became the stuff of media frenzy and the couple were married on the 18th of April. When Princess Grace produced a daughter (Caroline) in 1957 and then, to great rejoicing, a son and heir (Albert) in 1958, the fairytale was complete. Onassis and the scheming Tucker both had what they wanted and the economy of Monaco didn't look back.

In the 1950s, it may have been possible to have some romantic notions about the Riviera but that time is long gone. Non-stop development, much of it poorly controlled, robbed the coast of its isolated charm long ago. The tyranny of poorly built and poorly maintained apartment blocks and seemingly uncontrolled development in the surrounding hills, has left the place looking shabby and decrepit away from the main tourist places. None of this grim reality, however, seemed to be sufficient to dent anyone's enthusiasm for the Riviera's promise of eternal youth and a quick Euro and the hopefuls still flock there seeking fame and fortune. The night before we left Auribeau for the final leg of our journey, Jo drew my attention to Jim Ring's summary of the Riviera: 'Even though the reality of the Riviera seems daily to diverge ever more from the dream and the ideal, so powerful is this promise that the reality is ignored.'[24]

The Alps, in a broader sense, contain something of the same dilemma. So imbued are we with the idea of the Alps, that we overlook the crowding and pollution and have a limitless tolerance for the tourist-tackiness that is everywhere. Tourism has created the Alps in all but the physical sense. It is the bedrock of the economy and the tourist industry has made the people prosperous and shaped both their lives and their communities. Many visit the Alps and experience the place in that detached and vicarious way that tourism has of packaging the foreign and presenting it: stripped out and simplified. There are many Alpine towns that only exist in this way. They have been created from the first stone to satisfy a tourism need and the culture they present is in part a caricature, stylised to reflect the fashion. In the place where mass tourism was invented, tourism is the culture.

In the short time that it has been possible to travel the length of the Alps without crossing a policed frontier, the nature of tourism has changed. The Chinese are the next saviours of the industry and adaptation to this fresh reality is everywhere. But there is nothing new in this. The English may have come to the Alps first but their influence had waned by the early 20th century and after World War I, other Europeans and Americans became the important visitors. In more recent years, open borders across the EU have widened the range of tourists and the range of tourist pursuits. The locals adapted to the newcomers and the new ideas as they had adapted to the English, by learning new languages and providing what the customer wants. In the Alps, a layer of tourism has become part of the culture everywhere.

Despite all of this, the Alps do have one redeeming feature

lost to the Riviera. No one sitting on the beach at Copacabana or Surfers Paradise or Waikiki would give a second thought to the pebble beaches and flat seas of the Riviera. But there is no denying the mountains of the Alps their place in our hearts. They are simply stunning and so infused with our common history and threads of western culture and political systems that they can shrug off the worst efforts of the developers and tourists. The mountains make sense on their own, they don't have to be interpreted or moulded. They don't even have to be understood. They are there in all their magnificence and that is enough.

Our week of Riviera idyll also gave us time to gain a perspective on our own journey. We had, after all, managed to get from one end of the Alps to the other without much drama and, as bikers are libel to do, seen the place at a basic level. We had gone there looking for the best motorcycle roads in the world, looking for an untarnished alpine environment and looking for an understanding of how the mountains and the people who inhabit them had rubbed along. We had also gone there with as many preconceptions as it was possible to stuff into one set of saddle bags. Most of those had been discarded along the way, replaced by ... well, maybe just replaced by new misconceptions, still pristine and yet to be challenged. Our experience of travel has always been that culture, language and history are so bound up together it is difficult to forge understanding from observation. History is interpreted through the filter of culture and language and these have to be lived. At a practical level, trying to make sense of a place in which you don't belong is a fraught and risky business. Despite this, we believe it is important to make the attempt and to give our travels context. Even if we fail and never properly understand what we have experienced, the attempt to do so has at least fired our curiosity and there are few things more beneficial to our enthusiasm, and dangerous to our common sense and well-being, than an active curiosity, a fast motorcycle and a little time.

The mountains had, however, affected us deeply. It was not just the terrifying beauty of the place, mountains (and great deserts) elsewhere share something of that aura. What sets the Alps apart is the stories they contain. I have often said that the most beautiful place I have been was the Tanami Desert in north-western Australia. It is stunningly beautiful and frighteningly flat and empty. There is a place near the centre of that desert where you can stand on a slight hill and turn through 360 degrees to observe a flat horizon with no other rise in the ground and not even a substantial tree to break the line of ice blue sky. It is a place where you can feel your own isolation and frailty in your bones. But the stories of the desert are hardly accessible. They are ancient stories blown on the red sands and buried in the very earth itself. In the Alps, the stories are everywhere, often competing for your attention and always sparking curiosity. Some of the best stories can be found in the roads and railways that carried us through the mountains. There are roads built by Romans to link an empire, Hapsburgs to collect taxes, Napoleon to repay a debt, Italians to resupply an army freezing to death in the mountains, and roads hacked out, scratched out, by local communities trading between villages.

Then there are the modern roads built by cooperating nation states each more sophisticated and dramatic than the last, linking together a continent across both a physical and cultural divide. You can just drive on these roads if you like and that is a wonderful experience in itself. Or you can spend a little time considering the reasons they were built and the people who built them and those whose lives were changed by them. Looked at from this perspective, the Alps contain an unmatched density of stories, overlapping, intertwined, often contradictory, but always fascinating.

So, are these the best motorcycle roads in the world as John Hermann claims? Perhaps they are, and not just because of their bituminous contortions. These are great roads because they have more than scenery and engineering as wonderful as that is. These are great roads because they lead us to great stories.

The last leg of our Alpine journey in search of our last story was less than 50km along the old corniche past Nice and Monte Carlo with the Golfe de St Tropez as still as a millpond stretching out into the Mediterranean. It was a tedious ride through heavy traffic and within a few minutes we were wondering if it was worth the effort and if the handful of kilometres to get to the end would make any difference. We had, after all, started our exploration of the Alps in a search for great motorcycle roads and there were none of those around. Whatever our misgivings we pressed on into the late morning crush hoping that Menton would be more than the chimera it seemed and would have something to say to us; something to make sense of our own journey.

The Menton we found was a smaller resort town, clustered inside a circle of towering hills plunging down to the sea. The place was neat and well ordered and lacked the crowded feel of Nice and Cannes. It seemed less grubby and looked like the place you might go for a family holiday. The town's excellent winter climate had been noted by the middle of the 19th century when it had only two or three small hotels and a few villas and it was this feature that transformed Menton from a backwater to a lucrative gathering place for the dying. Much of this was the work of Dr James Henry Bennet, who had been born in Manchester, educated in Paris and practised medicine in London. Like many others of the time, Bennet contracted tuberculosis in his forties. He packed up in London, and moved to Menton in search of a cure. Other invalids sought out the good doctor and a roaring, if gloomy, trade in caring for the dying was soon the main economy of the town. While Bennet lived on for another 30 years, most of those who came seeking a cure were not so fortunate. It would be another 100 years before antibiotics were developed and widely used and before 'consumption' ceased to be a scourge. In the meantime, Menton would take up its palliative place on the Riviera; Cannes for living, Menton for dying. It was the grave of one of those unfortunates we had come to find.

William Webb Ellis had been the rector of St Clement Danes Church in The Strand, London and died of tuberculosis in Menton in 1872. We found his grave in le Cimetière du Vieux Château high above the northern end of the town. The place had a spectacular view. A few kilometres north the last limestone alpine spurline descended into the sea and marked the border with Italy, behind us narrow-gutted spurs rose sharply to join the main range at the end of the long march of mountains we had followed all the way from Slovenia. To the south, the main part of the town marked out a small plateau below the towering hills in orderly rows of red tiled roofs. It was a peaceful place and I sat for a long time enjoying the quiet while Jo waited with Just Sue. The grave was well cared for but said little about the man. I don't know if Webb Ellis was a good man, if he was a worthy rector to his church, if he regretted not marrying or if his last desperate journey to die far from home in this sunny, beautiful, awful place gave him any peace. What I and many others know of him took place in his early life when he was a student at Rugby School. It was there about the year 1823, while playing a game of football, and in complete contravention of the rules of the day, he picked up the ball placed it under his arm and ran with it. In doing so he gave us the essential feature of the game of rugby and demonstrated one thing we can all do in our lives: pick up the ball and run with it.

Endnotes

1. Fortey, Richard. *The Earth An Intimate History.* New York, 2004, Vintage Books, p 85.

2. Morris, Jan. *Trieste and the Meaning of Nowhere,* London, 2001, Faber, p 9.

3. Gilmour, David. *The Pursuit of Italy: A history of a Land, Its Regions, and their Peoples.* London, 2011, Allen Lane, p 266.

4. Ibid., p 264.

5. Thompson, Mark. *The White War: Life and Death on the Italian Front, 1915–1919.* New York, 2008, Basic Books, p 204.

6. Anonymous. *The Question of the Tyrol,* New York, 1923, Self Published, p 16.

7. Fukuyama, Francis. *The Origins of Political Order: From Prehuman Times to the French Revolution.* New York, 2011, Farrar, Straus and Giroux, p 135

8. Nathan Haskell translator. *Victor Hugo's Letters to His Wife and Others (The Alps and the Pyrenees).* Boston, 1895, Estes and Lauriat, p 11.

9. Symonds, Margaret. *A Child of the Alps.* London, 1920, T Fisher Unwin Ltd, p 14.

9. Ring, Jim. *How the English Made the Alps*. London, 2011, Faber and Faber, p 31

10. Ring, Jim. *Ibid*

11. Ring, Jim. *Ibid*

12. Twain, Mark. *A Tramp Abroad*. US, 2000. Digital republication by Penn State, p 207.

13. Ibid, p 208.

14. Waring, George. *Tyrol and the Skirt of the Alps*. New York, 1889, Harper and Brothers, p 103.

15. Ibid, p 108.

16. Ring, Jim, op. cit., p 121.

17–19. Codevilla, Angelo. *Between the Alps and a Hard Place: Switzerland in World War II and the Rewriting of History*. Washington, 2000. Regnery Publishing, p 45.

20. Twain, Mark, 10C. cit.

21. Murray, John. *A Handbook for Travellers in Switzerland, and The Alps of Savoy and Piedmont*. London, 1865, John Murray, p 378.

22. Hartley, Jenny (Ed.). *The Selected Letters of Charles*

Dickens, A letter to John Forster 1846. New York, 2012, Oxford University Press.

23. Murray, John. op. cit., p 379.

24. Ring, Jim. *The Rise and Rise of the Côte d'Azur*. London, 2011, Faber and Faber, p 3.

25. Ring, Jim. Ibid. Page: 272.